Cannabis Energy Medicine - 6 Week Map to Self-Healing © 2016 by Jamie Lynn Thomas.

Books may be purchased by contacting the publisher and author at CannaEssence, 12081 West Alameda Pkwy #480, Lakewood, CO. 80228; 720-316-0196 or by email at info@CannaEssence.org

Cover Design: Jamie Lynn Thomas

Cover Image of Jamie: Debra Neeley
Interior Design: Jamie Lynn Thomas
Publisher: A division of Amazon
Editor: Evan Thomas
Library of Congress Catalog Number:
ISBN: ISBN-13: 978-0692753675

    ISBN-10: 0692753672

1. Spirituality 2. Self Help 3. New Age 4. Metaphysical
First Edition, Volume 1

Printed in Charleston, S.C.

Heart String Dedications:

To All those shadow pack workers taking care of their stuff! One of life's greatest challenges is to hold our wounds close to our eyes & our hearts.

To my family, my clients, and students who support and teach me so much each and every day; Thank you for inspiring me to embrace my shadow pack, so that I can keep striving for the best me I can be in each moment. You all humble and astound me by your generosity, love and kindness. May each one of you go out and do the great work you are here to do with an elevated vibration.

Preface:

In 2000, I was out of action mentally and physically so much so that I was deemed disabled by the state of Colorado. I walked with a cane and was so disconnected from my body and mind that I would seem like another person at times. I was told that all we could do for my health was to maintain and work with the revolving door of symptoms and imbalances by adjusting medications. Our last hope was to combine some integrative therapies to see if that could shift some things.

Jamie Lynn & Zoe in the Field

In 2003, I formally started my studies in clinical flower essences after having been introduced to them from a herbalist healer who was working with me on my health issues in 2000. During this time, I was taking 50 prescribed medications a day and seeing over 15 doctors in various fields of specialty as well as being deemed 100% disabled by the state of Colorado. I was doing nothing but getting worse, feeling worse and seriously considering the reasons why I should stay on this earth. Until, I started using the essences, working with my nutrition, my intuition and harnessing the power of my sweet gifts of sensitivity instead of running away from them, I was a lost soul suffering in the crowd.

I walked this deep inner journey of transformation looking at the pieces of myself that caused me discomfort in my body or other senses. As the days, months and years piled on top of each other, I started to trust what I was being shown through this inner reflection. The essences gave me the ability to see all the suffering in others I was causing by my own imbalances from my shadow pack. We all have our own shadow pack. It follows us around, and we fill it full of the pieces of ourselves that we do not want to look at. Do not have the ability to do anything about it or just plain do not have the vitality or resources to uncover this buried box of something, it's just too painful or atrocious to see.

The use of the essences encouraged me to come back into my body and the present to reconnect to my heart and inner gifts. Now 15 years later, I'm a shining light of vitality and hope for my clients, apprentices, and peers. Walking this journey has taught me so much about the human desire to heal and live ones life's calling. Without this self-journey, I would not be conversing in the realm of text about a concept that will CHANGE YOUR LIFE. I took this self-information, and I applied it to my clients, students, friends, and family. I started to notice human patterns of imbalance and a real need for a set of essences that worked with human consciousness, colors and resonancy that stems from the heart space.

As I was healing, I noticed that my bioelectric field would grow and expand on days that I was working from the heart space. On days where I was depleted, triggered and imbalanced; I would sense a deep type of heaviness that would bog me down and increase my pain levels. I soon learned that I was losing my ability to resonate and harmonize with my surroundings by using my heart. When I recognized that the heart field itself could be measured by its bioelectrical output which is 100,000 more than the brain. I knew that it was time to stop living from my mental center and time to embrace the soft messy puddles of the heart space for that added 100,000 times potential.

Introduction:

The birth of CannaEssences are a blended marriage of color therapy, quantum physics and plant medicine all rolled into Cannabis Energy Medicine and VibroChromoTherapy. This co-creation was birthed out of love for the cannabis plant spirit, art, beauty and a desire to serve humanity. I was called to work with the images, vibrational essence, and colors of Cannabis plants. As my collective of practitioners and students studied these unique plants we found that each species (*you know those funny names that pot is now called i.e. Sharks Breath*) had its own unique vibration and a special message for humanity. Each new species was created with a shared intelligence with humans for a final goal or purpose, and that in itself holds great weight energetically. For where intention goes energy flows. Each species has been bred to be the best of the best. Very similar to the way champion purebred horses are mated with other pure breeds seeking out a certain trait i.e. longer running stride covers more distance due to longer body & legs. This same concept has yielded cannabis plants with very high vibrations due to this special breeding.

As I started to work with cultivation, then visiting others cultivation sites I felt like a sponge which was absorbing this whole new world of growing. As a lifelong green thumb and vegetable gardener, I was astonished by the different growing methods and the qualities in the vibrational frequency of each cultivation site.

I was called to certain strains and cultivations. I would sit with the plant from an early age all the way to maturity. I learned of its behaviors, traits, and qualities for six months. I did ethnobotanical research on high altitude mountain dirt grew cannabis. I found that each plant message seemed to have archetypical human behaviors or traits that were associated. Each plant's individual message, image, and personal vibration resonated with a specific color on the Manchester color wheel. When testing groups of students and willing friends or family we found that when a color was paired with an essence or image that was incongruent with that colors resonancy it created a disconnect in the product itself. That meant that each color has a unique mate or mates that vibrate at that frequency, and it can be seen under an electron microscope.

As a researcher and scientist, I continued to study the harmonic resonance and dissonance using quantum mechanics and an electron microscope. I was able to see the symmetrical water crystals when the essence and a color were paired harmonically. When they were not in harmony, a type of fracturing occurs, and the water crystals become asymmetrical or shredded.

I delved deeply into working with the essences in my daily practices, moving through pains in my body, emotions, odd ascension symptoms like dizziness, vertigo and more. As I worked my way through the color spectrum with a variety of essences, a group of 12 KEY allies presented themselves as an initial set to support others who are sensing shifts or wanting to encourage shifts in their consciousness, perceptions or just get to know themselves at a more intimate level. Cannabis as a plant encouraged and supported the shift into homeostasis whenever I was around these twelve rainbow healers.

This CannaEssence 12 Rainbow Master Set works with 12 key color spectrums that revolve around shades of green to balance, open, elevate and increase the frequency of the heart field: Lime, Green, Emerald, and Turquoise. All the other colors of the spectrum work with chakra zones and other body zones of the human bioelectric field. The other color you see in daily life are; Red, Orange, Yellow, Blue, Indigo, Purple, Violet, Magenta. This rainbow color spectrum that revolves around the powerful hearts bioelectric field yields a comprehensive system that works to balance the PEMS system with colors and energetic resonancy.

All essences work the best when you actively take a role in the healing process. I challenge you to take a look into the mirror and look into your shadow. Bring it out of the darkness and let it enter the light for you to look upon with compassion, equanimity, joy & friendliness. Let it serve you and humanity through service to yourself through heart centered self-reflection and observation. A ho!

Contents

Part One

VibroChromoTherapy

Vibro = Vibration or energy   **Chromo** = Color or pigment   **Therapy**= Treatment to heal

VCT (VibroChromoTherapy) is a collection or group of modalities that uses vibrations, energy, colors and pigments to self- heal a disorder

Vibrochromotherapy is a combination of vibrational imprints and color therapy to create a new form of resource for the human energy system PEMS or the Physical, Emotional, Mental and Spiritual bodies. The PEMS is especially important as color association works with the body-mind and the subconscious to transform the way we perceive the world and our part in it. While the flower essences specifically work with the entire PEMS or human energy system, the colors work to integrate the active, conscious mind and soul. When using color attraction, the PEMS system is naturally attracted to the color it needs most at that moment. It is very similar to actively choosing the outfit you will be wearing by your attraction to the color dominance or blending.

The Goal of VibroChromoTherapy is simplicity. Start with your color attraction and work your way through the colors of your choosing as you need them. My intention, like Bach, is to see a color set in everyone's medicine cabinet. This way each household has the tools to self-heal with color & picture attraction. VCT is so easy; you can add it to your daily routine without adding time to your busy schedule. CannaEssence is the first line that is working to further the research on VibroChromoTherapy.

"Everything is Energy" ~ ALBERT EINSTEIN

Chapter 1 **Energy Medicine**

"If you want to find the secrets of the universe, think in terms of energy, frequency, and vibration." Nikola Tesla

Energy medicine has become a broad term used to describe any modality that employs energy to create changes in the PEMS systems (Physical, Emotional, Mental, and Spiritual). There are two types of energy medicine in the scientific realm. One is an observable energy that can be seen and measured this is called veritable energy medicines. The second is considered to be undetectable or unverifiable energy that cannot be seen or measured this is called putative energy medicine.

Veritable Energy Medicine includes modalities like magnet therapy, light therapy, and color puncture (acupuncture using colors). Although many alternative medicine practitioners do not add electromagnetic resonancy techniques and radiation to the category "energy medicine" it is classified as a veritable energy. Putative energy medicine includes modalities like healing touch, reiki, pranic healing, spiritual healing, psychic healing, esoteric healing and shamanic healing. These two categories offer the opportunity to look at our perception of energy, frequency and vibration as a society.

In eastern traditions, both kinds of energy medicine are employed in hospitals and daily doctoral care. In the west, we have classified the energies that we can see and measure vs. the ones we cannot. It goes to show just how our western society views energy medicine. The biggest rebuttal is the lack of evidence and fear of the unknowns. Only in recent years have we been able to measure the bioelectrical output from organs and the physical body as a whole. As a scientist, I will wait for the day when we have the tools and machines that can measure the effects of putative energies on the PEMS systems.

"Anything considered spiritual or metaphysical is generally just the physics we do not yet understand." - Nassim Haramein

What is Energy Medicine?

"Conventional medicine, at its foundation, focuses on the biochemistry of cells, tissue, and organs. Energy Medicine, at its foundation, focuses on the energy fields of the body that organize and control the growth and repair of cells, tissue, and organs. Changing impaired energy patterns may be the most efficient, least invasive way to improve the vitality of organs, cells, and psyche." - David Feinstein, Ph.D.

Energy medicine to me includes all aspects of the PEMS system, the goal of the modality is to educate and empower. In this text, energy medicine is referring to any modality that uses energy to create changes in the PEMS systems. Energy Medicines can be a combination of veritable energies or putative energies or Vibro/Vibration Therapies.

In the east, the Physical, Emotional, Mental and Spiritual bodies are associated with chakras and auras or subtle bodies. Descriptions of chakras and auras go back to some of the earliest writings from humans. Currently, science does not have enough precise tools to measure these bodies to prove or disprove their existence. However, anyone can sense these energies with themselves or another person or animal. In chapter two, I describe an exercise that engages your sensory and awareness organs of perception. Once you are exposed to this type of exercise, you will be surprised at how much of your life is affected by energy.

Albert Einstein a German physicists created the formula $E=MC^2$ A formula we learn in grade school. You may remember that this is the theory of relativity or the relationship between energy and matter. If energy is affected by matter moving through space, then all types of matter can be affected by energy. Our PEMS is made of invisible coalesced energy and water. Our bodies are an electric circuit and each one of our cells, organs and tissues all emit a specific energy frequency fingerprint. Animals, insects and other forms of matter or coalesced energy all have a unique energy signature too.

An easy way to picture this unique energy signature is to imagine your personal fingerprint. Even if you are a twin your fingerprint will be uniquely yours. One hypothesis is that each fingerprint is created through the neuroelectric tension that pulls on the epidermis in the womb as well as the friction of the fingers on the womb wall. Fingerprints can be regenerated to their original state after having the epidermis, or top layer of the skin peeled off. This regeneration is thought to come from a type of biomimicry that is imprinted in the dermis in the womb. This means that the finger imprint has been stored deep in the skin between the muscle and nerves. Therefore, your unique energy field is just that yours and only yours.

If your bioelectric field is affected by your cells, organs, viruses, bacteria and your environment, would it be safe to say that your energy affects the energy around you in space and time just as much as the things around you affect your personal energy imprint? When you are sick or injured, your energy output emits a different energy frequency than when you are vital and vivacious. The Heart Math Institute studied the bioelectrical output of the brain verse the heart and found that the heart emits 100,000 times the frequency of the brain.

This study showed me the infinite potential of the heart field. If I could tap more into my heart to capitalize on the 100,000 x potency and stop focusing my energy in my mind, I would be able to unlock the mysteries of the universe and raise my personal vibration. Perhaps, help others to raise their vibration and that of their environment. In this way, each person could do their part to heal the world one frequency at a time. When you become aware of your personal energy vibration you create a bridge of intention to the PEMS system and a direct link to the heart fields power of frequency.

The Heart Math Institute took this concept and expanded it by doing global research on the Earths energies and frequencies relationship to environmental health and human population. This is why Cannabis Energy medicine like the CannaEssence are so valuable; they are built around the 100,000 x heart field and infinite potential frequencies. By using intent and mindfulness, you too can connect to your electric heart and benefit from that extraordinary power. Energy medicines will encourage you to heal the world from the inside using one intention at a time. To understand energy medicine and vibrational remedies, it is supportive to have a basic understanding of the elders in the field and their lineage.

Elders in Medicinal & Vibrational Remedies

"Energy Medicine is the future of all medicine." C. Norman Shealy
Founding President of the American Holistic Medical Association

The three most influential fathers of medicine are; Hippocrates, Paracelsus, and Hahnemann. Hippocrates 460 bc- 377bc is the "father of modern medicine," his well-known quote, "Do no harm" is famous for its use in Western medicines graduation ceremonies for new Doctors of medicine. Doing no harm was the foundation of my Vitalist training, and I have seen its threads in the alternative, complementary and integrative medicines. Vitalism is fueled by the life force of the person and is affected by the PEMS. Most alternative or complementary practices revolve around the principles that the body has all the tools it needs to heal itself if only we can provide a supportive environment for this cultivation. Hippocrates was the first to say that disease was not a punishment of the gods, but a product of your environment *(internal & external)*. He claimed that negative thoughts, environments, etc. could cause dis-ease in the body. This particular fact has been slowly lost through the evolution of Allopathic & Western medicine. However, in the past few years, I have seen a resurgence of Doctors referring patients for body-mind counseling and training as a tool for healing.

Paracelsus 1493-1541 was an astrologist & physician who openly burned books that did not support his claims or that spoke of treatments or cures that were detrimental to the body. He was the first to claim that like cures like or the law of similar. This concept is the basis of homeopathy. Paracelsus taught that the basics of medical science should be the study of nature, observation of the person sitting in front of you, experimentation and experience. He was also one of the first to start clinical studies with a control factor. By controlling factors of the experiment he was able to observe more accurate results. This type of experimentation yielded subtle but powerful medicines called homeopathy.

16

Hahnemann 1755- 1843, after his death his predecessors opened a medical college in his name in 1848 which has continued to thrive into the 20th century. He formally developed homeopathy, using Paracelsus concepts from 300 years in the past. He completed the picture of homeopathy by bridging the gap between the metaphysical and medical community. By creating a college that continued the clinical studies, observations of patient and nature he created a long lasting form of medicine that is thriving today. Hahnemann was the first to propose succussion (*hitting the solution on the palm*) as a way to enhance or potentize the remedy. Succussion is the basis of many liquid homeopathic preparation methods as well as trace amount dilutions. Hahnemann's research ignited fires of inspiration in Edward Bach, who created homeopathic remedies and birthed flower essences into the world less than 100 years later.

Some of our greatest principles have come from our forefathers and elders in medicine and other vibrational remedies. Hippocrates, Paracelsus, and Hahnemann all contributed greatly to allopathic and alternative medicines. As a proponent of integrative therapies, I see the validity and the desperate need to blend all aspects of what works for the person sitting in front of me. In my eyes, the term integrative therapeutics means that the practitioner is working in conjunction with all other practitioners for the benefit of the client.

Flower essences work with a person's soul expression in the body. When you are ill or experiencing discomfort in the body, it may be a reflection of a soul/body imbalance. Something is off, and the two are not seeing eye to eye. This PEMS imbalance or expression is where the essences come in as a valuable resource. Work with the colors, pictures or bottles that you are most attracted to and at your own pace. You will work through emotions and pain using two minutes of self-care, self-awareness, and flower energy medicines to support the healing and awaking process. All your work will create lasting changes in the PEMS.

As you continue to work on your PEMS system, you start to peel away layers that no longer serve your system. If you stop the process, the layers may start to rebuild and then you would have to do the work of peeling those layers off again until you were back where you once were; except you will have a higher level of vitality to continue growth & expansion. Rebuilding layers are the natural protective process for the body when it is experiencing suffering without receiving support in return. It creates a callus or shell that protects the delicate transforming caterpillar within until the shell is ready to be cracked open to expose the butterfly to the world.

When used in combination with other modalities or resources the essences can provide a crucial framework of support for the healing journey.

Peeling and layering create a synergistic effect where all formulas and self-work are added to the vital foundation of healing. This approach, in my practice, has yielded shocking results of transformation and ascension of symptom pictures and conditions. The main challenge for most folks when using essences is to use the information they receive to move up and out of what is no longer working for them. This allows you to ascend literally by rising from a lower plane of existence or vibration to a higher plane of frequency. Looking upon tthe shadow pack is dependent upon the person's ability and desire to complete self-work. For many people it causes greater suffering to look upon the highlighted shadow of themselves. I believe this is one of the reasons why essences are challenging to study. The measurements to test self-work are far from comprehensive and are far from accurate at this point in scientific evaluation.

This can be subtle to the person who is in the midst of this transformation. In a therapeutic relationship, we can more accurately gauge self-sufficiency and awareness, but even then this is the objective view of an observer. The power of the inner healer, who communicates with mindfulness to the entire system, is part of the inner journey to self-awareness as well as the external articulation process that many others have pioneered. This path has been created for future generations to walk, expand, pave and eventually turn into a super highway of self-healing. When we take into account the information of the past, present and the effect on the future; we take into account all facets of a topic. Holistic thinking of the PEMS is how essences have woven themselves into the fabric of healing. Anyone using energy medicine can be thankful to the three most influential fathers of medicine Hippocrates, Paracelsus, and Hahnemann.

*Free Download Link – Bach Flower Essences for Beginners e-Book

Universal Energy Principles

What is Universal Energy?

Universal energy, in this text, is the term used to encompass the numerous forms and paths of known and unknown energies. Universal Energy or Vibro energies unite by clumping together in a pool or vessel. A vessel is a tool that coalesces the energy into a single working unit. Vessels activate this stored energy by transmuting the energy unit into spaces where it can be of the most use to Universe. As human vessels or containers, we naturally are filled with Universal Energy (UE). Some vessels have learned to maximize their relationship with UE and have raised to higher levels of consciousness. Some famous examples are Buddha, Ascended Masters, Elder Shamans and much more. You have the vital potential within you to embrace your UE and elevate your conscious experience too. Unlock the potential within your spaces.

Everything is made up of energy that vibrates at different frequencies. As our understanding of the universe increases so will the tools to measure energy frequencies. Very similarly to the way we once thought that the world was the center of the universe and flat. Now we know we are, but a dot within an infinite number of other dots coalesced into dot clusters or galaxies. Is all we need to do is continue to dive deeply into universal energy, who knows what discoveries are next.

Recent studies on the human bioelectric field have shown that the esoteric aura is the bioelectric field. Taking something that was considered metaphysical and highlighting it with science. This has revolutionized the way that energy work has been viewed by the allopathic establishment and hospitals. In 2016, JCAHO or the Joint Commission on accreditation of healthcare organizations included modalities like massage therapy, healing touch and Reiki to be part of all surgical insurance packages. This means that energy work has become the standard of care just like in the East.

Everyone can sense and use universal energy for their self-healing process. This is one of the principles behind Reiki and other energy modalities. Heal thyself and then heal the world. Healing from the inside out. Each of us can use UE as a way to replenish our PEMS and as a cleaning and balancing system for the self-healing process. UE is a tool that allows you to help yourself and others regardless of belief or dogma. Universal energy gives you unlimited accesses to Source/Science energy's & Devine/Magical (Magic something science has not worked out yet) without the rituals or incantations. You only need to be self-aware and open. As we talk more about the PEMS & Ascension, we will talk about how to use your natural gifts as well as Universal energy with special self-awareness tools = CannaEssences.

In the holographic theory, in the matrix or foundation of the universe, exists a place called the multiverse. This is where everything in each of these holographic dimensions intersects. There are many strands of energy woven into the multiverse bridges and paths of energy that connect "everything" together through its spaces. There are many mystical and ancient names for this bridge quality, it can be found in all cultures all over the world, some examples of bridge locations or names are a tree of life, pillars of life, Aztec temples, Mayan sacrificial temples, and the great pyramids. This is why Sacred geometry is so integral to the building blocks of the universal energy frequencies of UE.

The Earth has ley lines covering the planet's surface with coalescing energy nodes where two ley lines meet. A nexus or increased energy node is where ley lines cross or meet. These are frequently associated with places of power like Stonehenge, and the pyramids. Some of these bridges have been thought to be power nodules where someone with the right consciousness can unlock the gate and walk the bridge to the other side. It is hypothesized that the-the multiverse and its infinite universes within are ALIVE and conscious. Full of energy pathways or meridians that infuse the physical matter with it lifeblood its life spark of energy frequency.

Types of Energy

When drawing in any energy from the UE field, it is helpful to ground deeply in the heart space and engage that 100,000 x power. When you have grounded UE in the heart space, you will able to clarify your intentions while being very specific about the use of the energy. This allows you to make monumental changes and raise the vibration of yourself and the environment around you. It has been taught in many traditions that the misuses of light energy attract karmic retribution, corrupting entities, and other dimensional beings. Old judgments say that Goodness and Innocence also tend to attract evil and dark energies.

In many traditions, there is the light vs. dark mentality. Placing judgment and preconceived notions on those who use the light or the dark for their purposes. Light energy has been associated with: all Joy, Compassion, Goodness, love, life and light in the multiverse. Light energy's heal and can be drawn from the UE field or called on from the ready and waiting for sources around us.

"Dark energy can also be referred to as that which does not serve you or other. Therefore in the Peruvian traditions, it is referred to as hooch or heavy energy. This heavy energy serves as compost for the earth. That which does not serve self may serve something else in the universe". - Jamie Lynn Thomas

Dark energy in old traditions has been considered the sum of all hate, oppression, evil, cruelty, absence of light and Dark Matter in the Multiversity. Chaos and dysfunction fall into the dark energy category. Dark energy can be used to heal or to harm. In this book, it is used to understand that ascension symptoms are rooted in shadow pack hidden by darkness. Dark energy is a powerful self-healing tool when used with compassion and good Intention. Dark energy, when used for light, will be products neutrality and balance as seen in self-healing. Old judgments say misuse of dark energy attracts, karmic retribution, evil good entities, and other dimensional beings.

The East uses the image of the yin-yang as a symbol of the perfectly balanced PEMS system. Half the circle light and half the circle dark, with each half having a piece of the other within its circle. For example, the while half of the circle contains a small circle of darkness. This is the visual representation of all Universal energy and how each side requires the other to be healthy balanced beings contained within a vessel. We are after all just coalesced energy radiating our conscious choices into the universe, either raising or lowering your vibration and the world around you.

"Energy is Energy. The outcome depends on your Intentions, determining the final energy frequency and vibration." – Jamie Lynn Thomas

What is Ascension?

The definition of ascension means to "rise, to mount, go up" in different cultures & religions this term holds other connotations. Ascension, when discussed in a metaphysical manner, is referring to planes of consciousness or planes of existences which are present in different dimensions. When you raise your vibrations in your bioelectric field, you are rising from a lower plane of existence to a higher vibrational frequency, consciousness or plane. This means that when humans ascend in a literal form on the Earth their perceptions of their human experience have shifted. The act of ascension awakens those to their true spiritual nature or their higher purpose or calling. For clarity, Ascension in this book refers to the spiritual awakening process that many awakened souls are experiencing on the planet at this time.

What are Ascension Symptoms?

Ascension symptoms are about the process of spiritual ascension, spiritual awakening or the evolution of a newly expanded consciousness for the human experience. Ascension symptoms are an expression of your soul, heart, and consciousness expanding in your physical body. This can cause dis-ease, discomfort, and disconnect from the awakened consciousness of your higher self. During this time of new consciousness, your body is being upgraded, connected & retuned to a higher frequency. This is where old patterns of being, doing and living are coming up and asking to be shifted. Some patterns of ascension symptoms are showing up in allopathic medicine as symptoms with unexplained physiological reasons as you can see below.

If you have 5 or more of any of the symptoms below you are most likely experiencing ascension or awakening.

- *Need for personal space, personal time*
- *A sense of urgency that time is running out, but you do not know why*
- *A sense or knowing that something is happening or changing in the world around you*
- *Changes in hearing, odd tones & pitches that come & go – tinnitus like symptoms*
- *Cold & flu symptoms that come suddenly and leave as suddenly*
- *Extreme sensitivity to others energies and emotions*
- *Feeling invisible or separated from certain patterns of thoughts, people or negativity*
- *Feeling like you are in a dream world at times*
- *Feeling more drawn towards nature, outdoors, plants as a place of solitude*
- *Feelings of frustration, rage, irritability or judgment that come out of the blue*
- *General body aches, pains & tension that are not caused by exercise, injury or work*
- *Increased self-awareness & inner talk or body awareness*
- *Increased sensitivity to scents or smells. Sometimes smells appear out of the blue come & then go*
- *Increased sinus, ear or eye issues or sensitivities*
- *Odd Digestive, GI patterns that have purgative effects that come & go for no reason*
- *Odd headaches, dizziness, vertigo patterns that have no physiological cause*
- *Odd skin changes that come & go without cause – rashes, hives, itching, tingling, creepy crawly sensations*
- *pooling of fluids in the body that create heaviness or suffocating sensations in the limbs chest or back*
- *Pulsing or prickly sensations on the head, hands, legs or toes*
- *Sensing other entities, persons, or shadows around you – seeing things out of the corner of your eye*
- *Sporadic bursts of creativity, inspiration, and enlightenments that cause frantic creations*
- *Sudden increase in synchronicity with people, places, circumstances i.e. 1:11, 11:11, or other recurring #'s*
- *Sudden sensitivities to foods, chemicals, plants, products, etc. that were fine once but no longer are*
- *Super sensitive to sounds, pressures, winds, lights anything that touches the physical body*
- *Unexplained nervousness, anxiety or thoughts*

Why Use CannaEssences to Work with Ascension Symptoms?

CannaEssences and their easy color attraction system allow the sensitive, intuitive, empathic person to communicate with their internal physician. This internal physician can communicate with all aspects of the human bioelectrical system. This would include all aspects of the PEMS and the direct connection to a source or your understanding of your higher self.

The Three I's & UE

As you start to work with UE (universal energy), let's consider Imagery, Imagination, and Intention. As you work with Ascension, Ascension symptoms and your shadow pack you will want to pull from your toolbox full of the three I's. When you use the three, I's to work with your shadow pack you will always be supported wherever you are if you use these three basic tools. I discuss the ones important for your six-week journey in Part Two of this book. Below I have included some easy exercises to get your PEMS to engage with the three I's.

Imagery

Everyone has experience with imagery when you are a child. This is built into the fabric of childhood and slowly lost over the years as you move closer to an adult. Our society encourages imagination in our youth but dismisses it in adulthood. If you are attracted to Cannabis Energy Medicine you, most likely, have a knack for imagery. As you start to work with your PEMS, you may start to engage more of your brain by using the three I's.

When you use the CannaEssences for self-healing, Imagery will help clarify which applications you need in that moment. By using imagery as a tool, it helps to create a therapeutic relationship between all aspects of your PEMS. In essence creating a bridge for your PEMS to work with each of these centers individually. In essence creating a therapeutic relationship with yourself. By using Universal energy principles like the three, I's it will help to keep you in a balanced therapeutic relationship.

An easy way to start working with the Cannabis Energy Medicines or the CannaEssences is to use Sacred geometry, the building block of the universe. When using UE & CE, Imagery takes the form of Sacred Geometry, colors, and other imagery in practice. Some symbols like sacred geometry are very useful for the beginner; however there are many other symbols, patterns and images you will encounter in this unique work. Some other examples include tarot card decks, VibroChromoPictoGraphy cards, Reiki symbols, Sanskrit ancient symbols and glyphs. Choose the form that you are most attracted to create a bridge to imagery. In part two of this book, you will be educated on the use of VibroChromoPictoGraphy.

"Imagery is the laying on or use of patterns using imagination and Intention. As you move further into personal ascension your ability to read, understand and apply Sacred Geometry and symbolism will expand and grow; thus giving a clear picture of you personal PEMS needs." Jamie Lynn Thomas

Imagination

Imagination is the bridge between Imagery and Intention. Imagination is how we take Universal energy and translate it into a usable focused tool. This is also how we can work with our PEMS highly intelligent internal physician.

"Imagination, when used with Cannabis Energy medicines, will help bridge the gap between the known and unknown." – Jamie Thomas

Imagination allows you to access all of your PEMS and the Universal patterns in your bioelectric field. Imagination allows you to sense instead of feel. Sensing uses descriptive words and feeling uses emotionally charged words. By using sensing or imaginative terms to describe the sensations in your PEMS you will be able to sense when your vibration is higher or lower than it was the last time you checked. By sensing more deeply, you can act with focused intention leaving the wild universal energies around you alone. Harness, Focus, Release

Seeing or Imagining in the mind's eye (3rd eye) strengthens the effects of your self-awareness and personal consciousness. By sensing and imagining, you can more fully see all the layers of your bio-electric field. By cultivating your *imagination* similarly to how you would caretake for a garden from seed to fruit, you will encourage your senses to increase sensitivity and frequency. As you continue to ascend from a plane of lower vibration to higher vibration, your sense power will elevate your self-healing to the deepest levels of your intention.

Intention

    The intention is the focused goal or plan. In alternative healing traditions, intention is the term used to bring awareness to the healing process. *The intention* , when used with UE, gives us a path to completion and continuation. Set the intention with consciousness and self-healing will come in time. Please be fluid in your *intention* with ascension work, as the *intention* can change mid-session as the layer peels away and a new layer asks for new resources to grow. Continue to check in with your PEMS so you can refocus on the new areas as needed. Do what is right for your self-healing path and work with your shadow pack using active PEMS listening and intention. Support the resistance + increased vital resources = ascension from a lower plane of existence to a higher plane.

"Intention is the most powerful of the three I's in the therapeutic relationship. Healing occurs in a space of intention". Jamie Lynn Thomas

    The intention is the setting of goals or intended conclusions that are brought into the field through shared intention in the therapeutic relationship. *Pure intention* is to serve the person in front of you from the 100, 000 x powerful heart space. This is best done from the heart field and will allow deep work in the conscious and subconscious areas of Ascension.

    All forms of healing use some combination of the three I's to create long-lasting changes in the PEMS. I invite you to start to use the three I's in your everyday lives. How can you increase your vibration by activating your superpowers of Imagery, Imagination, and Intention?

Chapter 2 The Human Bio-Electrical Field and the PEMS System

The human bio-electric field, in this text, is referred to as the PEMS – physical, emotional, mental and spiritual fields which incorporate all the astral or auric bodies. As the heart is the largest resonating Organ, measured in the bio-electric field, we specifically work with the heart to activate this 100,000 times power of the brain to get to the core of total body healing. Each one of the CannaEssences works with the heart to open, soften, angle, activate, soothe. They create balms of safety for the sensitive ascending soul in this new world of human consciousness.

The human bio-electric field is still in its early stages of study as we have only just begun the ability to measure the theoretical principles of our elders. It is only now, in the quantum era, that these new devices are emerging to measure this sensitive system. We hope that our work with the essences as individual essences and with our clients, friends and family will lend to the research on vibration, color, and other energetic type medicines.

"In a few decades, scientists have gone from a conviction that there is no such thing as an energy field around the human body, to an absolute certainty that it exists. Moreover, science is explaining the roles of energy fields in health and disease. The main reason for the recent change in outlook is the development of sensitive instruments that can detect the minute energy fields around the human body." James Oschman, PhD

PEMS System

The human PEMS system consists of the Physical human body, Emotional body, Mental body and Spiritual bodies of a person. A visual representation of the PEMS is shown in the picture to the right. The PEMS, when calibrated with

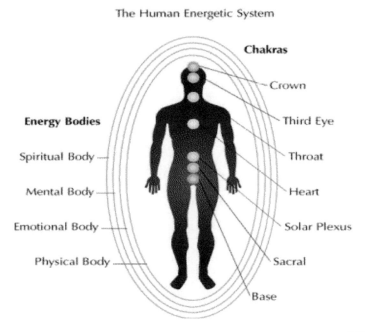

The Human Energetic System

Chakras
- Crown
- Third Eye
- Throat
- Heart
- Solar Plexus
- Sacral
- Base

Energy Bodies
- Spiritual Body
- Mental Body
- Emotional Body
- Physical Body

the hearts intelligence and bio-electric field will balance each one of these systems. This is a unique way of thinking of the PEMS systems for it leaves it all in your control of your association or attraction to what this term means to you. In the book, we are referring to these bodies or their representation in the human life expression.

For example, when thoughts circulate in my mental body I sense them in my physical body as a heaviness and inflated energy in my head. Therefore, my thoughts are affecting both my mental and physical bodies. Physiologically, there is a complex nervous system in the heart called the "heart brain" that interconnects the heart & the brain with its two-way superhighway.

The best way to get connected to your PEMS is to use the foundational body-check as a daily exercise. In a day I may perform the body check exercise up to 20 times depending on what I am doing for the day. When I see clients, I am checking in with my body before they show up, as they show, multiple times during the session and after the session. This allows me to know exactly what is going on in my PEMS and what I was sensing from the client. This type of exercise clarifies you from other. It is the most valuable exercise in this entire book. It starts and ends each and every exercise or protocol. As you work with the PEMS and the body check you will notice how different people and places make your PEMS feel.

For empath and highly sensitive people (HSPs), this exercise will serve to empower your gifts of sensitivity. In my journey as an HSP, I found this exercise to be required to get through a day without taking on other people's stuff. You can too. Use the six week plan to create a new habit that serves your sensitivity. Learning what is serving your PEMS and what needs work, phased out or removed completely.

Body Check Foundation Exercise

Body Check Exercise – Step 1 to Connecting to Your PEMS
Take a moment to get in communication with your body mind by performing the body check. This is a great exercise to get you to connect to your PEMS so that you can be fully aware of the changes your body goes through as it delves into body talk.

Body Check Starter Questions:

You can simply start by asking the body a few questions:

1. Body mind we are listening, please tell us what you want us to know?
2. Is there an area of the body that has discomfort, pain?
3. Is there something in your life that is causing you suffering? If so where do you sense this in your body?
4. What area of the body is affected when you talk, think or imagine this thing that is causing you suffering?
5. When you sense into this area what information do you get?
    1. Audio, visual, scents, emotions, pain, inner knowing, sensing's, flashes, movies, etc
6. Ask this area what type of support it would like?
    1. It may flash a color of the essence, touch somewhere on the body –ANYTHING really – no expectations just listening
    2. <u>If it is not a direct answer</u>
        - Look at the four CannaEssence color boards and use color attraction using touch

Exercise- Body Check Steps 2 & 3

1. Body Check EXERCISE Part 1- to ground & connect the body
1. Close your eyes or keep them open in a soft gaze

2. Do a quick inventory of the entire body- breathing in the body as a whole for three whole body breaths

3. Then start with your attention at your feet breathing in for 1 or 2 breaths then moving onward upward to the head Once you are complete you are ready to begin body check part 2

2. BODY CHECK EXERCISE #2: to move heavy energy & get in full body mind space
Step 1: Imagine there is a large vase full of a warm honey-like fluid that is being poured gently over your head in a cleansing and nourishing movement that will eventually be pooling at the feet & soaking into the great earth mother as sweet compost

That which does not nourish us can nourish the mother – our hoocha (heavy energy) is her black gold!!!

The honey acts by taking everything that is not serving into itself to be fed as ambrosia to the earth

2. **Step 2:** As it moves its way slowly down the body it pools and sits on areas that need a little extra attention or nourishment – breath this into your body letting it leave you clean, bright, clear and full of life

   If there is a pain in an area – allow the honey to pool around the area. Seeping in bringing with it the light of your awareness. Bring your breath and awareness into the area. Breathing through it for three breaths and on the final breath exhale deeply letting your awareness float on to the next area with the next breath

   Step 3: The honey has reached your feet & is now pooling around you slowly seeping into the earth. You see this dark & heavy honey leaving your body & it is transformed as the earth sucks the ambrosia of hoocha. I image a brightness of diamond golden rays as the earth mother transforms the hoocha honey. She transforms darkness to light and uses it to grow her inner gardens. She loves our heavy energy & wants to co-create a more solidified PEMS for you for it also supports her too.

 *Free Download Link –MP3 Audio of the body check

Kirlian Photography & the Bio-Electric Field

Kirlian photography is a type of contact print that uses high voltages to render the images or coronal spheres that are put off by the plasma discharges that are present in people, objects, etc. This particular type of photography uses physics principles to display the

Ordinary Tap Water

Energy Water

bioelectric activity or health of the image being produced. Kirlian photography's first experiments can be traced back to the late 1700's with scientists like Georg Christoph Lictenberg and Nicola Tesla working with their understanding of these principles and its effect upon humanity. Kirlian Photography did not come into the mainstream until Semyon Davidovich Kirlian and his wife Valentina dedicated 30 years of their lives to the study of this fascinating imaging system. Semyon Kirlians name has been synonymous with Kirlian photography from the founding date in 1939. By 1970 he had become so well known due to his published book, Psychic Discoveries behind the Iron Curtain. The importance of Kirlian photography, about, essences is the coronal ring that is present with each essence or plant that has been measured.

When two items are compared using Kirlian photography we find a pattern that displays that the brighter the light that is produced means that this item has a higher vibrational frequency than something that has a duller, thinner or weaker coronal image. The brightness of the image tells us the health of the object being photographed. When the object possesses bright, vibrant colors, full or expanding colors that can be blinding in areas; this brilliance speaks about the inner vitality or energy that is present. For a less active or healthy example, we see it expressed with a change in colors that are more muted, less vibrant and dull. Let's take a drop of ordinary tap water verse energized water and see what happens when the two are exposed to Kirlian photography. Just like Masuru Emoto Messages in the water we see energized water, which is water that was taken from the same tap and then put in a glass to sit in the sun's rays for a minimum of 5 minutes. In the example above, you can clearly see that the right image of the energized water has a brighter more vibrant Corona than the ordinary tap water on the left image.

The 38 Bach Flower essences have been studied in great detail, for the past 60 years, by the Bach Institute. In Mechtild Scheffer's book, The Encyclopedia of Bach Flower Therapy she

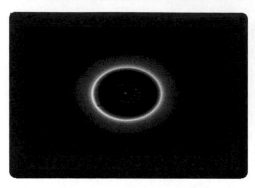

displays all 38 remedies via their Kirlian fingerprint. She noted that each essence held its unique patterning that no other essence contained or resembled. To the left is an image of a drop of Oak flower essence. She postulated that every plant, flower and human has their unique vibrational fingerprint that can be measured by Kirlian

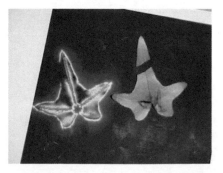

photography, auric readings, and highly intuitive people.

Severed leaf with whole Bioelectric field mirror image

This unique energetic fingerprint can be seen even when a piece of the subject has been severed. For example, a pristine freshly picked leaf has been cut leaving it free of one piece of its body. When placed under Kirlian photography we can see the phantom image left behind by the bioelectric field. This means that even when a limb is severed the system still holds the original imprint of the perfect and pristine wholeness. In the shadow box example below, you can see a cut leaf next to the pristine or whole projected Kirlian or bioelectric field fingerprint.

This type of image led to many studies looking into phantom limb syndrome and the

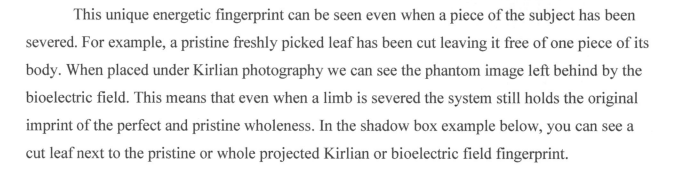

bioelectrical implications on long-term health and mortality rates. However, these studies were not all controlled, nor did they have large enough groups to get accurate statistics, so a call for more research between the bioelectric field, our ability to measure it and its impact on human health longevity is needed before a scientific mind would accept the above postulations as facts. Therefore, we need to take an open-hearted and willing perspective as we go into the future of studying the bioelectric field accurately, instead of just metaphysically.

Cannabis has been studied using Kirlian photography but only in a visually or artistic manner. Our goal with our CannaEssence sets is to have each plant tested for its whole plant

Kirlian fingerprint as well as taking Kirlian fingerprint images as Mecthild Scheffer did with the Bach flower essences. The first image below on the left is a Cannabis leaf that well into flowering with falling fan leaves. The second Image is of a leaf taken from the plant and left to wilt 30 minutes while preparing the unit. The leaf to the right and most brilliant is taken directly from a plant in the height of its life just before it started to flower. Can you see a difference in the health of the plant just by its Kirlian fingerprint?

Notice that the bright white, blue and indigo colors that are present in higher frequency plants that yield a healthier plant.

Can we translate to humans? Not by scientific standards. However, there is a time when each one of us has noticed a person for the light that they shine into the world. Do you know someone who always lights up a room? Do they ever look brighter, happier or more vital to you than other people? I wonder if we put these highly energetic people under a Kirlian photograph, what would their Kirlian fingerprint look like?

Kirlian Photography and Auric field therapies had combined to gives folks a bit of a translation for what colors mean when Kirlian photographed. In the example below from Bespoke photography at Full Spectrum Presentations, we see a set of human hands that have been labeled with a variety of metaphysical, Traditional Chinese Medicine concepts and body-mind awareness techniques that give us an example of the importance of our hands, colors, and our self-awareness.

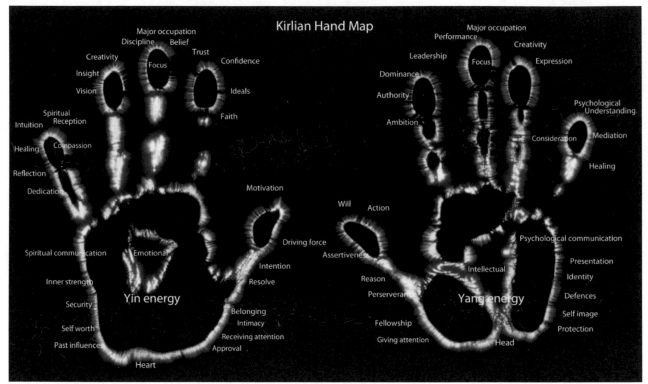

Kirilian photography continues to deepen its ability to interpret and facilitate higher resolutions through bodies of science. As our knowledge of the human bio-electric system expands; so does our ability to create devices that can more accurately measure the bio-electric field. I hope to encourage more focused research on human and plant bioelectric fields.

Aura Anatomy

The aura or bio-electric field is the seven layers of our PEMS system. A good way to image the auric field is to imagine your body like a Russian nesting doll. These are the dolls that fit within the larger sized doll. Traditionally there are seven dolls that fit within each other, coincidentally mirroring our bioelectric field. A good way to look at the auric fields is to go by chakra colors and terms. Chakras are areas of coalesced energy where we interact with different aspects of our PEMS. Chakras start at your feet and finish 1-4 feet above your head or crown. Each chakra has dominate traits and attributes that support or highlight the shadow pack. Each chakra is associated with a specific body of the auric or field. For more detailed color descriptions see Chapter five, VibroChromoTherapy.

The first chakra is the root chakra or etheric body it is the closest body to our physical body. It is associated with the color red. The second chakra is the sacral chakra or emotional body and it is represented by the color orange. The third chakra is the solar plexus or mental body and it is seen as the color yellow. The forth chakra is the representation of all the heart chakras and is known as the astral body correspond to the color green, while the lateral or side heart chakra is color purple . The fifth chakra is the throat chakra or etheric template for our higher self, it is linked with the color blue. The sixth chakra is the third eye chakra and is known as the celestial body and is connected with the color indigo. The seventh main chakra is the crown chakra and is known as the causal body where we connect to source and is associated with the color violet. I was unable to include an image of the chakras and causal bodies in this text, however you can easily google aura anatomy to see an image of the description above.

To play around with sensing your own aura or that of another person you can use the form below to conceptualize your imagination and imagery that may come up. I like to use crayons and colored pencils to sense into my PEMS. You will be surprised at how much information starts to come into your system when you mindfully engage with the bioelectric field.

Have you ever noticed any areas on your body or of another person where there is heat coming off of them? When you get close you notice it is only coming out of a small areas perhaps their shoulders and the rest of them feels neutral temperature. This was you sensing into someone's aura. Now go ahead and try this exercise once with yourself and once using another person. Walk them through the body check and use your PEMS senses to map out their auric field.

Draw Your Aura Exercise

Name: _____ Date: _____

1. **Are you currently experiencing any of the following?**

Pain/tenderness ❏ No ❏ Yes: **Stress** ❏ No ❏ Yes: **Allergies** ❏ No ❏ Yes **Depression** ❏ No ❏ Yes **Numbness/tingling**

❏ No ❏ Yes: **Stiffness** ❏ No ❏ Yes: **Recent surgery** ❏ No ❏ Yes: **Swelling** ❏ No ❏ Yes **Mental suffering** ❏ No ❏

Yes: **Emotional imbalance** ❏ No ❏ Yes: **New Consciousness** ❏ No ❏ Yes **Anxiety or Fear,** ❏ No ❏ Yes

2. Perform a body check before your start drawing. What do you notice in your PEMS? Please note any physical, emotional, mental or spiritual imbalances you are experiencing in the space & body below or in your minds eye.

Draw Your Aura & PEMS Sensations Below

Draw your aura & body sensations with the crayons provided. What colors do you sense in your fields?

Burning   Tightness or discomfort   Ache   Sharp Pain   Numbness   Other   Aura/field =Holes, hot/cold spots, movement, etc.

=====   oooooooooo   xxxx   ////////   *****   zzzzz   *You Fill in with colors or drawing*

3. **Which color or colors are you most attracted to?** *Circle below*

Green	Purple	Violet	Red

4. I suggest doing a self-session with the corresponding color and then rechecking in with your aura & PEMS systems with the body map below.

After

Burning	Tightness or discomfort	Ache	Sharp Pain	Numbness	Other	Aura/field Holes
=====	ooooooooooo	xxxx	//////////	*****	zzzzz	*You Fill in with colors or drawing*

Energy Center & Chakra Quiz

1:(7pt) Name to the color

Word Bank

1. Heart _____
2. 3rd Eye _____
3. Solar plexus _____
4. Root _____
5. Crown _____
6. Sacral _____
7. Throat _____

Red

Green

Indigo

Violet

Yellow

Orange

Blue

2:(2 pt) Stability, Grounding, the physical, are traits of

A: Green/ Heart
B: Red/ Root
C: Violet/ Crown
D: None of the above

3:(2pt) What one sub-Chakra did we talk about and the corresponding anatomy

A: Purple / High heart
B: Yellow / Lateral heart
C: Purple / Lateral heart
D: Green / post 3rd Eye

4:(2pt) Spirituality, Wisdom, Understanding Are traits of

A: Violet / crown
B: Green / Heart
C: Red / Root
D None of the above

5:(3pt) List three facts about the heart Chakra

_____   _____   _____

6:(2pt) What two colors support the heart chakra?

A: Violet / Green
B: Green / Purple
C: Purple/Violet
D None of the above

7(2pt) Throat & 3rd Eye Chakras are best represented by

A: Truth / Vision
B: Thymus / Thyroid Problems
C: Blue / Indigo
D: all of the above

Answer Key is at the back of the book

Chapter 3 Flower Energy Medicine & Flower Essences

Edward Bach History – "Father of Flower Essences."

Edward Bach was born in 1886 and died in November 1936. He was an Immunologist, bacteriologist, pathologist and physician. As well as a highly gifted intuitive with the ability to observe nature and the interrelationship with emotions. He was a thriving medical doctor who held many positions in the hospitals of London from 1912- 1922. He was the founder of the nosodes, a fecal bacterium remedy used in homeopathy. In, 1917 he suffered from severe abdominal cancer and was not expected to survive. He was given three months to live and was told to say his goodbyes and get his affairs in order. He took a sabbatical for a few months and moved to a secluded country home and started to work with nature to find a cure to his terminal cancer. During this time frame, he continued to see patients from his thriving practice as well as consult with fellow Doctors from all over the world.

In, 1928 Bach founded the first seven flower essences in the world. The essences were used according to personality types, emotional patterns and the effects that these had on the human body. The set started with 7, 12 and then the last 19 essences were added. Bach worked clinically with the essences as the only form of treatment for many hopeless medical cases. He saw "miraculous healings" that he attributed to the human spirit being able to express fully in its physical form without hindrances from the emotions. He proposed emotions as the root of disease in the body. He then supported his theories with hundreds of case studies and curing.

"The action of the flower essences raises the vibration of the being…. They cure by flooding the body with the beautiful vibrations of the highest nature – in whose presence there is the opportunity for disease to melt away like snow in sunshine" Dr. Edward Bach

As he reached the end of his life, he was concerned that some of his works might be too radical for the public to take in on their own. He instructed that his secretary burns all his work after he died. He was confident that future generations would come to the same conclusions he did; that plants in nature can offer us healing and growth. It is sad that Bach, near his death, feared that his work was too advanced for humanity at the time, and anything that was not published was lost to the flame. This sad fact is the reason why so many people around the world have worked to further the research of Bach and other essences that are being created from plants and practitioners all over the world.

 *Free Download Link - Edward Bach's Heal Thyself eBook

How Are Traditional Flower Essences Made?

Sun Method   Boiling Method

The Sun Method is the Most Common:

Directions: *Use clear glass and tweezers if you'd like or a leaf from the plant itself. Sit with the plant and ask permission for medicine. Pluck flowers with tweezers or hands covered in a leaf to protect and keep separate your vibration from that of the remedy you are trying to make. You can also place flowers still attached to plant into the bowl of water. I tend to cover the surface of the water with the most precious & vital flowers leaving the wilting or day old flowers to turn to seeds on the stalk.*

Let the flowers sit in direct sunlight for a minimum ½ hour up to 24 hours. Usually, 4 hours is a good average time for powerful essences. I look for the bubbles in the water & the wilting of the flowers. Early morning tends to be the best for making

flower essences. Being out in the early am keeps the bugs out of your water as they are not usually flying around till 11am-12pm. Watch out. Bees are attracted to the flowers.

Boiling Method:

The boiling method was used for the 3rd group of 19 Bach essences. Bach said that they needed this level of boiling to transform. This method was used as a symbolic nature of transformation. Bach believed that to truly transform your emotions, and pains in the body, you must move into another form of being. Ascension.

Directions: *Collect ½ pot of stems and flowers and leaves. Add water to make the pan ¾ full. Boil for a ½ hour, strain, and use to make stock bottles as with the sun method.*

Essence Terminology

Mother bottle: Is the pure essence (*right out of the infusing bowl*) mixed ½ and ½ with brandy. For example- I have 2 oz of mother I add 2 oz of brandy to create my Mother bottle or essence.

Stock bottle: is made from 1 dropper full of the mother bottle then filled the rest of the bottle up with brandy. Bottles you buy in the store are stock bottles.

Dosage Bottle: *(what you give to the client or self two weeks or one month dosing)* is a ½ oz dropper bottle filled with 1-4 drops of stock essence in spring water.

-I like to add a touch of brandy or glycerin for added preservation just in case I want to carry the bottle around for the month in my pocket, purse, etc. You can also use hydrosols in place of the spring water to add a special something to your now flavored essence with yummy herbal hydrosols. Some good carries are: Spearmint, peppermint, lemon balm, rose, rose geranium, sweet orange blossom, and cannabis.

Succussion: Hitting on the palm to "potentize" or increase potency. I've also heard of this technique as the activation principle to the remedy. Some belief in doing succussion of a remedy 108 times to finalize potentization. Some remedy makers do not use this method at all.

Sacred Geometry & Flower Energy

"We are Conscious Sacred Geometry experiencing itself" ~ Jamie Lynn Thomas

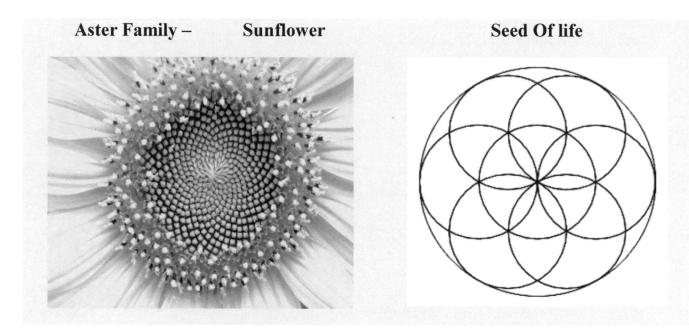

Aster Family –   Sunflower   **Seed Of life**

Sacred Geometry & CannaEssence™

Sacred Geometry & all flowers are integrated at the level of the plants DNA building blocks. As you can see in the above example of a sunflower, in its geometrical design it holds the pattern of the flower of life within its center. This is not uncommon in nature. In Keith Critchlows' book on the Hidden Geometry in Flowers- Living rhythms, Form, and Numbers, he highlights that every garden has hidden sacred geometry present in the flowers themselves. He postulates the higher intelligence of the nature of creation and touches on sacred geometry which he states is present in everything we do as humans. This is important to the use of the CannaEssences as each essence was infused with three sacred geometrical designs that support human consciousness: The Seed of Life, Flower of Life & the Tree of Life.

The Seed of Life:

Seed of Life and the Seven "Days" of Creation
As strange as it sounds, the Bible mimics correctly
this geometric procession

The Seed of life is said to contain all the building blocks for everything we can see or perceive in the Universe. This would include biological life forms, material objects, nature and so much more. The seed of life contains limitless potential.

The Flower of Life:

The Flower of life is said to be a tool to help reach spiritual enlightenment. It has been seen in many cultures and religious temples. It has also been a predominant image that we have seen in crop circles. The flower of life is said to hold the "void of life" which holds in a container all the building blocks of all creation. Leonardo Da Vinci's journals have multiple images and formulas built around sacred geometry and the human form. The flower of life was thought to be a foundational formula that may hold potential for time travel and limitless energy production.

The Tree of life is seen in many cultures throughout the ages. The concept that one tree holds all the wisdom of the universe as well as serves as a doorway into all other trees' of life, cosmic dimensions, portals or planes of consciousness. The tree also serves as a metaphor for how a tree changes, grows, gets injured, looses limbs and still keeps on growing an expression of our physical or human form on this earth. Some believe that the wisdom in the tree of life can be translated into the human body through spiritual ascension or awakening.

By using sacred geometry in our everyday lives such as meditation aids, in quantum physics, our religious temples and all of the Nature we begin to see the importance of these three images in the world around us and within ourselves. We believe that we can understand the meaning of the universe through sacred geometry like fractals or the seed, flower or tree of life. That is why we combined the high vibrational potency of Cannabis with matching frequency colors and sacred geometry. By deeply connecting with the plants and ourselves we have co-created a form of support that the human energy system has never seen before. This unique framework has set the tone for healing at a deeply transformative level. Rise Phoenix out of the ashes and shine your true form of light!

What Principles Are Behind Essences?

"Energy is the prime mover of all we see and know. You change the energy, and your body has to respond."
- Christiane Northrup, MD

Quantum physics tells us that the world, universe and everything in it are just coalesced energy that is perceived as solid but in reality is just energy held together by bonds that never actually touch one another. These bonds are held together through an attraction or repellant nature that leaves space for each atom and its smaller parts the proton & neutron, neutrino, etc. Therefore, in space nothing ever touches, and there is more space then there are things floating around in it. This is some of the groundbreaking research that Nassim Haramein is doing. He has proven; with mathematically sound formulas, that the space between each atom holds limitless potential. He has called this space, "black holes" these are present between every single atom of the universe. This means that within each atomic bond there is space between itself and its neighbor. Within this space, there is limitless potential to move from one black hole to another. He has proposed that this is how we can physically and ascend into space. He dubs this new consciousness our opportunity to travel literally into space, new dimensions and planes of consciousness. He surmised this through logic, the study of sacred geometry, the study of Nature, and physics.

An easy way to wrap your mind around this concept is to think Star Trek. Some aliens can easily travel faster than the speed of light with thought alone. $E = MC2$ is the formula that describes this type of thought & travel. The theory of relativity tells us that energy, matter & the speed of light are all interrelated, and this is what Nassim and other physicists are proving right now. They postulate that intention carries energy and, vibrations, therefore, where intention goes energy flows this is the basis of the law of attraction.

If we take the above science into account, we see that our forefathers of medicine were awakening to the infinite possibility for humanity through their understanding of the Universe around them. By learning the building blocks of the universe and creation, humanity can explore the rest of the Universe and the billions of galaxies that are present within the interconnected matrix. The most important thing to note is that each of these enlightened people studied Nature and listened deeply to their body and inner knowing. By doing so, they tapped into the power of the heart space and infinite space to create changes in the PEMS. By combining this with the intelligence of water, intention to create healing opportunities for self-care we create powerful vibrational remedies. The law of attraction allows each person to be attracted to certain flower essence sets opposed to other sets or flowers.

Water is a living being. It is intelligent and can be affected by our thoughts and impressions. When we use intention, we tap into that intelligence to co-create a vibrational imprint of the selected plant, color, image, etc. Masuru Emoto author and researcher wrote Messages from Water Vol. 1 & 2 the Hidden Messages in Water, which sold over 400,000 copies worldwide. He proves that our thoughts, spoken words, and perceptions affect the molecular structure of water. To the right is a picture from his book that shows the molecular structure of water after he exposed it to a prayer, thank you, you make me sick/I kill you and love & appreciation. This is extremely important as our bodies of

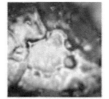
Water Molecule, Before Offering a Prayer

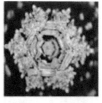
Water Molecule, After Offering a Prayer

Thank You

You Make Me Sick, I Will Kill You

Love and Appreciation

composed of 71% water and it has been proven that our thoughts can affect our bodies. By infusing waters with energetic imprints or energetic impregnations, you create intelligent water that wants to continue to co- create harmony and homeostasis in your bodies' waters!

The body/mind/soul connection is clearly something that must be cultivated so that optimal health can express. This means that if you become more aware of what messages you are sending to your internal waters, then you may be able to catch patterns of imbalance before they cause deeper suffering. Therefore, if you work with your internal waters and heart space your bioelectrical field expands, and you become a harmonic resonance & tuning fork for others who are vibrating at a lower frequency. By working on yourself, you start by dissolving imbalances in your waters by elevating them with programmed or balanced, neutral energy that gives the entire system clearer vitality.

*Free Download Link – The Hidden Messages in Water

Chapter 4 Cannabis Energy Medicine

"When Your Energy vibrates at a frequency that is in direct alignment with what the universe has been attempting to deliver your entire life, you begin to live in the flow and true miracles start to happen." Panache Desai

The Endocannabinoid System

The Endocannabinoid system is a bridge between the body mind that has been built into our anatomy and physiology of the human bioelectric system. The endocannabinoid system is constantly striving for homeostasis or a completely balanced human in all their body systems. Endocannabinoids also work as regulators where different body systems intersect or interrelate. This allows the endocannabinoid system to communication with various body systems, and cell types always motivated towards homeostasis. Endocannabinoids' are present in the human body whether or not you have ever used cannabis. They can be found in the brain, organs, connective tissues, glands, and immune cells. This is extremely importantly in the understanding of why physiologically the body can be affected by the changes in consciousness.

"As we get better at understanding how little we know about the body, we begin to realize that the next big frontier in medicine is Energy Medicine."
Dr. Mehmet Oz   The Dr. Oz show

Why Cannabis?

Cannabis as a plant spirit supports the human system physically with our internal endocannabinoid system. Spiritually the Cannabis plant has been used to find a new consciousness or reality with its hallucinogenic compounds. As a cultivator plant, Cannabis has co-created a unique relationship with the human spirit. We have focused on the female plants as medicinal allies. We have worked with the genetics of this plant to highlight desired traits and remove traits that we dislike or that are not serving the cultivation of this plant. While we have focused on these aspects of the plant we have seen a relationship develop that is one so unlike any other relationship that humans have with plants. Therefore, the Cannabis/Human relationship is extremely unique. Factor in the intentions of this daily interaction to ascend spiritually and expand your heart consciousness! Can you sense the unlimited potential?

"Energy work is priceless. It makes every day extraordinary and transforms the mundane to the holy." -Silvia Hartmann

Who Should Use the Essences?

These essences contain trace amounts of brandy and are glycerin based (99.9%) so that children, animals, elders, alcoholics could use the essences without any concern. We encourage you to look at the set. If you are not attracted to any of the colors or pictures, then the set may not be for your system at this point. We encourage you to check back with your system in a month and check for color or picture attraction. Most folks will be attracted to a color or picture immediately. We encourage you to follow this attraction towards your vital potential!

The First Cannabis Energy Medicines

CannaEssences are the first cannabis flower essences on the market. They were made to connect the *PEMS* at a quantum level by integrating color association and vibration attraction through the images on the bottles. Each cannabis plant spirit has a unique message, so these 12 are just the beginning of a larger line of plant spirits or devas whose mission is to help sensitive souls and support the ascension of humankind. They specifically work with those who are awakening to the new human consciousness and may be experiencing ascension symptoms. They are especially unique as they combine vibrational remedies with the color association, which was inspired by the Manchester color wheel studies, to create a new type of resource: VibroChromoTherapy.

How Will I Know Which Essence is Right For Me?

Is all you have to do is choose the color or picture that you are most drawn to. The awesome thing about the CannaEssence set is that it was built around color and picture attraction. Since the endocannabinoid system is constantly striving towards homeostasis, the essences activate an internal dialogue with the PEMS. This allows you to access directly your internal physician who can guide you to PEMS re-connection and self-healing.

I encourage you to start by looking at the image above and choose the first color or image that attracts you. This is the simplicity of using color and picture attraction. By the law of attraction, you are getting exactly what you need at that moment by using the colors or picture that you are most attracted or drawn towards. Some colors you may have an aversion to. This is normal to have some colors or pictures that you have resistance to or a dislike. Over time, working with the first colors you are attracted to, will allow your system to balance itself through thought the endocannabinoid system towards a state of homeostasis. When you follow the color attraction system, you will naturally work your way through the rainbow of colors and flowers as you raise your vibration. This will all happen at your pace if you allow your inner vitality to express and support your goals of self-healing. In part two, I give you a six-week map to self-healing that can be used repetitively until you reach a state of higher self-awareness and understanding.

Once you have chosen the color you are most attracted to, turn to the CannaEssence Monographs for more details later in this chapter. Each monograph includes a standalone self-application to support daily use of Cannabis Energy medicines. In Chapter five, VibroChromoTherapy, color therapy monographs are included for your reference and review. In Chapter Fifthteen, specific cannabis energy medicine protocols and applications are discussed using the master flower core four essences.

"Energy is your body's magic! It is your life force. You keep it healthy, and it keeps you healthy. If you are sick or sad, shifting your energies feels good. When you care for these invisible energies, it makes your heart sing and your cells happy!"

Donna Eden

Grounding / Red

Short Red CannaEssence Monograph

Red CannaEssence is grounding and energizing

Useful for:
- Feeling depleted Mentally & Physically.
- Root chakra is balancing.
- Meditation.
- Useful for low energy or exhaustion.
- For caregivers, working with the death and dying process.
- Helpful for the end of life stages.
- Helpful for body workers to develop healthy boundaries.
- Useful for communicating over long distances.
- For hangovers/vertigo/dizziness.

Red as a color is very grounding and works to balance the root chakra. Bringing in new refreshing energy into your light body through your pelvis, sacrum, and skull. This essence gives passage to the dark side of ourselves where the deep self-work and shamanic work are done. It connects you to your root source so that journeys are possible at new and unexpected heights due to the PEMS grounding effects. If you are experiencing ascension symptoms like vertigo or dizziness using this essence for 2-6 weeks is very supportive. Use this essence to ascend your present form.

Long Red CannaEssence Monograph

Species or Strain: Shark's Breath

Indications or negative qualities: Useful for low energy folks or those who are exhausted or depleted mentally and physically. For those melancholic or depressed situations in life, shaman work esp. underworld travel support. For caregivers working with the death & dying process, for the end of life stages, symptoms of interdimensional travel hangovers which result in signs of vertigo and dizziness. Use for any type of transition phase, a desire to see the shadow or the hidden aspects of the universe, for those needing to communicate over long distances of time and space.

Positive qualities:

-This essence gives passage to the dark side of us – our past lives and those who do shaman work for self or others

-Gives the support for transitions for those in the end of life this essence helps them sort out their death rights & unfinished business with the support of seeing the shadow that's not worked in this life or past lives.

-This essence offers a way to travel multiple dimensions with ease to the next life or next steps on your life journey

-connects one to the DARK MATTER OF THE UNIVERSE where you are interacting with the universe in a quantum manner

-Gives one the ability to communicate over long distances to the past and futures selves – use this as a tool to the break the mold and transform yourself at the deepest levels of your atomic makeup

Affirmations: Ascend your present form

Key Words: Low Energy in the Physical & Mental bodies, for any type of transition phase, Supports travel stability & self work, shadow work, grounding - Ascend your present form, fatigue, weakness, energize, rejuvenate, balance, powerful, end of life, stimulating, joy, love of life, creation of life, end of life, stability, security,

Combo with:

-Blue- Durban Poison: to co-create with your Akashic records

-Turquoise- Blueberry to melt the heat/ fire that was released when working with the red essences. If you experience discomfort in the body after using the red use the blue for an equal amount of days until you feel balanced again

-Green-

-Green> purple > red> yellow to create metamorphic changes using color therapy

Suggested body applications:

1. *To stabilize an out of phase PEMS -* apply to the back of the AO for balancing vertigo, dizziness, spinning or perceptional changes or other **signs of inter-dimensional time travel hangovers**

Key:

AO = Atlantooccipital joint – located at back of the neck where you bend backward at the crease

Plant Information: A tall, sturdy 5-6 ft plant by 1-2in stems and big stalks. Lots of colors predominantly red and maroon. It shines red when the sun's rays go through the leaves. The leaves filled out the rest of the plant are large and driven without light to that part of its body. Large fan leaves green-> purple -> red -> red yellow. Deep forest stank to it\light 1st notes and deep base notes with a light, heady quality to finish it off. Top leaves are purple – deep first

Suggested VibroChromoTherapy Color Board Uses:

Use the red board to work with Red, Green, and Turquoise

-Daily energetic hygiene exercises

-Color gazing or -Auric infusing

-Meditation aid

Red

Abundance/ Green

CannaEssence

ABUNDANCE 5

Short Green CannaEssence Monograph

Green CannaEssence is abundance and prosperity.

Useful for:

- Heart chakra opening & protecting.
- Meditation.
- Who want to desire to manifest abundance, prosperity & joy in their lives.
- Who have lost faith in the world or themselves?
- Helpful to shift depression.
- Supports protected heart opening.
- Supports learning & integration of that knowledge.

Green as a color is supportive to the heart. It allows the heart to feel a sense of peace, joy, and abundance from deep inner sources. As an essence, this green CannaEssence is full of prosperity, joy, and safety in the world. This essence uplifts opens and supports the sensitive heart. By resonating from the heart, you have 100,000 x more power than the brain to transform the world around you with your super heart powers!

Long Green CannaEssence Monograph

Species or Strain: Eisenbaur

Indications: Lack of joy, lack of prosperity or abundance, unable to see or desire abundance, lack of luster, lacking safety for the heart, having trouble learning lessons that have been taught before, over the hardened heart with barriers or walls, not being in the present due to armoring or judgment. For those who have lost faith in the world or themselves. For those who only see the negative or are pessimistic. For those who do not have the strength or desire to care

Positive qualities:

-The ABUNDANCE FLOWER

-An essence full of potential to see prosperity, abundance, joy and safety in the world. Allows this to come and bath them in a web of safety and protection as they cultivate this new home of potential and abundance – Let go of what was and see the possibilities of tomorrow

- Flower of SAFETY- a haven for "Everything's going to be all right."

-Essences of the air and ether

-Full of life-giving properties and toxins – a yin-yang essence without judgment or sway towards one or the other works with the Male-Female within each one of us by allowing the heart to melt and open to the possibilities of what will come. Making sure that the journey provides neutrality that neither is good or bad, but just is. Yin & yang without the judgment

-Activates the heart center so that TRUE JOY may be felt and that you can connect and resonate what is TRULY JOYFUL FOR YOU out to the world through your heart fields - Bring love and potential into your heart

-An essence that radiates the goodness that is here in this heartfelt moment

-MANIFEST PROSPERITY - Goodness will manifest with this essence

-Allow the progress others have made help you learn from their mistakes/successes

Affirmations: Manifest Prosperity!

Key Words: jealousy, depression, worn down, loss of faith, apathetic to suffering of others, armored, pessimistic, reawakening, abundance & joy, revivification, heart opening, heart softening, heart melting, protective, safety, lessons, relearning, retaining lessons, potential, love, uplifting, nourishing,

Combo With:

-Lime- to work with the archetypical Mother/farther & Green to work with the inner aspects to morph your perception & interactions with these types of figures within and out in the world

-Lime- To add to the sense of security and safety while cultivating openheartedness potential, mental clarity on your prosperity and abundance path

-Red- To give fire and vitality to the process of opening one's heart – Use for those who have given up the strength to care

-Red to balance an out of phase PEMS esp. after interdimensional travel – compress the back heart space with Magenta & the front heart space with Green

-Violet- To add a bit of vitality while calming the overly fired up souls

-Magenta on the posterior as a compress to open the back heart space

Suggested body applications:

1. Compress the heart space *(directly over the heart on both sides)* & chest with green on the front & Magenta on the back – directly behind the heart
2. Apply directly from the bottle to the heart space
3. Auric infusions to sooth an armored heart- do for six weeks to transform your interactions with the world. Accompany with the body check as always ☺

Plant Information: A bushy heavy kola plant is growing up to 7 feet tall and cola weighing at least 1-2 ounces a piece. The plant itself takes up a bit of space and will gently weave its overladen stalks through the neighboring plants. This plant has a ton of mica and other minerals and rocks in the soil near it high up in the mountains. Heady, very sticky and full of high, middle and base notes that linger on the high end

Suggested VibroChromoTherapy Color Board Uses:

Use the Green board to work with Red & Violet

-Daily energetic hygiene exercises

-Color gazing

-Auric infusing – Red vs. Violet Vs Green – check out the difference in your system or 1 before/after

-Meditation aid- To get into a heart centered space of pure potential & joy

Green

Destiny's Calling/ Purple

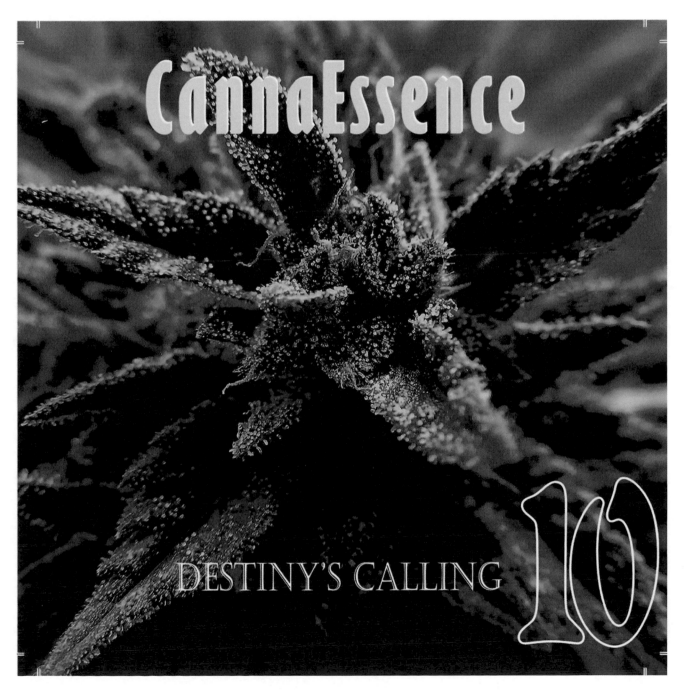

Short Purple CannaEssence Monograph

Purple CannaEssence is your Destiny Calling.

Useful for:

- Gently open & balance your side heart chakras.
- Meditation.
- Trust in spirit.
- Trust in your chosen path
- Supports your destiny, hear its call.
- For overactive mental & physical bodies.
- Faith in self and other is returned, be your lion heart.
- Helps to focus, prioritize, set & complete goals.

Purple as a color is supportive to the side heart chakras and encourages relaxation. As a CannaEssence the purple is full of clarity at the moment with the ability to give one fine-tuned focus towards calling. If you choose this essence as your #1, you are moving forward into your calling and the universe want you to know you are on the right track. You just need a bit of support to ascend to higher levels of being. This essence is pure trust in the universe and the path you choose to walk in this life. Find clarity from your story and let that nourish your lion heart!

Long Purple CannaEssence Monograph

Species or Strain: Purple Kush

Indications: For those who want to focus and talk to their body or cells. For those with excessive energy in the upper body and limbs. For those who are rigid and overly structured. For those who want to work deeply with their self and shadow. For those who have a vulnerable heart. For those with ear challenges that arise for no reason. For those whose, life pressures are weighing them down. For those who demand much from themselves with harsh criticism and judgment. For those who need to focus and prioritize. For those who are living in the future with much worry about this impending future. For those with overactive mental & physical bodies.

For those who have lost faith in their calling or spirit. For those who have lost sight of their goals but want to get them back

Positive qualities:

-Good for changing things on a cellular level – microscopic

-Supports your innate ability to go deeper and deeper into your core essence with ease, calmness, and confidence. Will work with what's up or it can easily get into deeper levels by dropping into intention where focus on the microscopic levels can occur- Great for self-work

-Focuses energy by allowing the system to calibrate with the earth. This allows pooling and draining of stuck or excessive energy to flow down the limbs into the earth

-Works deeply with the "vulnerable heart chakra" that is bilateral under the armpits

-Directly affects the ears – cranial plates esp. the temporals and the Eustachian tube

-The pressures of one's life are removed – Pressures of life melt away

-Helps one to own the demands they put upon oneself. Allows you to slow down and come back to the present = HOME

-An essence that helps focus with a keen eye on what is most important for the task at hand

  – What will serve me to do right now in the present?

-An essence that comes in and allows those who are hard workers to let down their guards and take in the love with a sweet embrace. This can soothe the *overactive mental and physical bodies*

-An essence similar to beech whose intolerance for others is created out of an overactive metal body – stopping any transference of own self-reproaching and judgment from others back towards the self for a balanced CLEAR and REALISTIC look at what was creating the judge imbalance

-An essence similar to impatience where it is all about speed with a focus on the need to judge others for their inaccuracy and inability to do the job the way I would like it done. Why not do it myself

– this essence helps balance this inner time clock to allow for the truthful unfolding of time and accomplishment this essence also allows the goals and expectations to become realistic so that one is reaching goals and moving on to bigger better ones with ease

-CLARITY IN THE MOMENT

-TRUST THE UNIVERSE & the PATH YOU have chosen to walk

Affirmations: Trust Spirit & your chosen path

Key Words: Trust, spirit, chosen path, destiny, calling, rigidity, unfolding, realistic perceptions, imbalance, judge, overactive mental body, overactive physical body, let down, relaxing, calming, balm, inability, love, embrace, slowing down, presence, vulnerable heart chakra, cranial plates, temporal, Eustachian tube, microscopic, cellular levels, universal energy, pressures, demands, unleashed, unpaged, free, soaring, focused, intolerance, impatience, need for speed, inner time clock, truthful unfolding of time, path, walking, trust in spirit, Confident, supported, nourished, relaxed

Combo With:

-Blue to support throat chakra activation

-Indigo- to support connection to self & source

-All heart colors- Green, Emerald, Lime, Purple, Turquoise, Magenta and Blue

-Violet – to balance the shifting and growth that occurs in this space

-Magenta- to integrate any changes made in the system

Suggested body applications:

1. Heart space- Anterior (front) - Apply a compress to the front of Green & Emerald to the heart, Lime to the upper heart and Turquoise to the upper heart. Purple to the side hearts chakras directly under the armpits. This will calibrate the heart and communication centers

2. Heart space- Posterior/back apply a compress of Magenta to the back heart chakra space and along the shoulder blades outlining the "wings" of your light spirit

3. Apply a compress to the top of the head with Indigo & Purple

4. Apply Purple as a lotion, compress or cotton ball application to side heart chakras or heart space under the armpits

5. Apply the cotton ball method - Purple and Blue to the heart space on the front and back of the body to activate the inner heart and ground it with spirit and your chosen path – Add Indigo to support courage through transformation

6. Total Heart Space Calibration- Do 1 - 6 and apply blue to the throat and apply along the midline to the perineal (*space between anus and genitals*) or umbilicus (*belly button*) ask the client which is preferred by the body/system

7. Apply as the cotton ball method to the lobes of both ears and down the neck 2-4 inches to support cranial plate shifting, ear infection clearing and dizzy sensations

Plant Information: Tall plant bushy wand reaching to the sun, tall plant with huge calyxes and little buds in the shade. Below on the stem, they have vertical veins with darker green as if that was the highway for the nutrition of the entire plant. Sweet floral notes and citrus scent orange calyx's purple fan leaves and purple and green stripped calyx's

Suggested VibroChromoTherapy Color Board Uses:

Use the Purple board to work with Yellow & Lime

-Daily energetic hygiene exercises

-Color gazing

-Auric infusing – Yellow & Lime

-Meditation aid- To move between dimensions

-Open communication aid for groups, workshops or teachers

-Chakra balancing & calibrating

-Heart chakra – Working with your vulnerable heart space – cultivating trust in spirit

Cleansing/ Violet

Short Violet CannaEssence Monograph

Violet CannaEssence is deeply cleansing.

Useful for:

- Meditation.
- Use in rituals or any occasion that requires a connection to source.
- Deeply cleansing & rejuvenating.
- Supports decreased pain and body awareness.
- For those who have experienced much change needed to integrate it into their systems.
- Communicate directly with source.
- Use on the 3rd eye, sacrum and ears for chakra activation, balancing & cleansing.
- Good for transitions of any kind.

Violet as a color is part of the light spectrum that is almost out of our vision and encourages us to look to yourself for the answers. Once you are deeply connected to the PEMS, you can easily communicate directly with the source of all things. Your world is about ready to become much larger as you open yourself up to the conversations happening all around you. This essence supports the integration and mops up of the process of growth and expansion. A great transitional remedy is waiting to help you join the movement of re-connection with your PEMS. Helps develop clear and realistic goals with focus and universal support.

Long Violet CannaEssence Monograph

Species or Strain: Master Kush

Indications: For those who want to communicate directly with source. For those who are looking for a place to start with the essences. For those who are feeling imbalanced due to big shifts and changes in their life or bodies. For those who use their mental bodies and mind to the point of fatigue. For those who are highly influenced by astrological and planetary alignments. For those whose dislike mornings. For those who require support to move through tough places of being. For those experiencing resentment, anger, hatred or frustration in their bodies. For those with stability and knee challenges. For those who want to interact directly with their soul. For those who have experienced much change, growth, and transformation in their systems, but need a way to integrate them into their system. For those who need to clear base levels of their systems so that they can more easily integrate higher vibrations and octaves. For any out of balance bioelectric system

Positive qualities:

-Uplifting and calming setting one in their body, so they more easily communicate with their soul

-Feel as if in communication with grandfather sky - coolly watching WITNESSING my transformations

-Cultivating inner growth

-Working to harmonize planetary imbalances for those struggling with an excess due to an astrological alignment i.e. mercury in retrograde

-Helps to balance morning rhythms, giving the system support to move through hard places of being. Uncomfortable spots – feeling distress or discomfort in the body

-Helps you be comfortable and being in the unfolding of discomfort with ease walnut like qualities

-Allows resentment to move easily out of the system feeling supported on stable legs with the knees made stronger

-THE SOUL GROWTH FLOWER - To open and use all your resources available to you

- Melting the heart allowing what was once shut down open to new possibilities. This essence allows this new heart puddle to pool around the entire body in a soft and gentle manner. Soothing the system making the heart a pool melting in the wake of a warm hand as if chocolate truffles that melt deliciously to fuel the sweetness of life

-A MOP UP FLOWER – for use after clearing big changes in the system or moving big things in the system

-Clearing base levels so you can use the other essences to hit your optimal potential in time and space

-Chaos = light & newness

-Trauma, triggers or shocks this is an essence that nourishes the out of balance system

Affirmations: Find comfort in the discomfort of growth

Key Words: Uplifting, mop up flower, chaos, newness, change, trauma, triggers, potential, movement, transformation, Integration, heart softening, pooling, melting, hardened, hallowed, hatred, anger, jealousy, brick wall, clearing, baseline, source, angles, guardians, communication, awareness, resentment, forgiveness, distress in the body, discomfort in the body, avoiding being in the body, renew, refresh, rejuvenate

Combo With:

-Yellow- to balance the PEMS

-Orange-   Deeply cleansing to self and environment

-Lime for those who have difficulty feeling anything or are apathetic supports softening of the heart in a gentle manner

-Indigo- courage to continue in the face of suffering

Suggested body applications:

1. This is the #1 Essence starting place ☺ Easy for many systems to take in the essences and start the changes that they will bring with their reflections and support

2. Use the quantum broadcasting method to prepare the bioelectric field and environment for higher levels of vibration – A great thing to do when you get your set for the first time

3. Apply with the cotton ball method to the tips of the ten fingers and toes as well as the 3rd eye

4. Apply Indigo and Violet to the crown and 3rd eye point with the cotton ball method. Compression if indicated. Sometimes a building or pressure sensation may be felt, if this is so, apply the violet to the back of the 3rd eye

5. Apply Violet to the bioelectric field for one month straight by doing daily drops in the water and spritzing daily then work with lime for the next month

6. Apply Violet to lower back heart chakras to open & soothe all the heart centers – Located From T-12 through S-3

Plant Information: 7 ft tall plant 1 in stem with broad top part of plant is very heavy with buds and they are turning purple first dotting the leaves with purple-hinged with green. Neutral, but fragrant aroma full of conjuring in the minds eye. The plant has a cohesive look among all other plants from this batch of seeds. Arms wide and full of embraces of safety and love. Seems to support all the other plants in this biosphere. Creating its own ecosystem within its small colony.

Suggested VibroChromoTherapy Color Board Uses:

Use the Violet board to work with Yellow & Green

-Daily energetic hygiene exercises

-Color gazing

-Auric infusing – Yellow & Green

-Meditation aid- To move between dimensions

-Chakra balancing & calibrating

-Clearing base levels of imbalances to prepare for higher vibrations

Violet

Chapter 5 **VibroChromoTherapy**

"Color is energy made visible." —John Russell

VibroChromoTherapy

Vibro = Vibration or energy   **Chromo** = Color or pigment   **Therapy**= Treatment to heal

VCT (VibroChromoTherapy) is a collection or group of modalities that uses vibrations, energy, colors and pigments to self- heal a disorder

Vibrochromotherapy is a combination of vibrational imprints and color therapy to create a new form of resource for the human energy system PEMS or the Physical, Emotional, Mental and Spiritual bodies. The PEMS is especially important as color association works with the body-mind and the subconscious to transform the way we perceive the world and our part in it. While the flower essences specifically work with the entire PEMS or human energy system, the colors work to integrate the active, conscious mind and soul. When using color attraction, the PEMS system is naturally attracted to the color it needs most at that moment. It is very similar to actively choosing the outfit you will be wearing by your attraction to the color dominance or blending.

The Goal of VibroChromoTherapy is simplicity. Start with your color attraction and work your way through the colors of your choosing as you need them. My intention, like Bach, is to see a color set in everyone's medicine cabinet. This way each household has the tools to self-heal with color & picture attraction. VCT is so easy; you can add it to your daily routine without adding time to your busy schedule. CannaEssence is the first line that is working to further the research on VibroChromoTherapy.

"Everything is Energy" ~ ALBERT EINSTEIN

In chromotherapy or color therapy there are positive and negative states of color. This is the reference to how people experience the color yellow when in a positive and healthy state. The negative qualities are the shadow side of the color being expressed as a negative and unhealthy state of being. I see the negative qualities as an indicator that these folks need yellow. They are deficient in this color or essence saturation. If someone is balanced in yellow they, most likely, will not need as much of the essence daily to make changes to their PEMS. This is why color and picture attraction work so well. You're automatically attracted or repulsed by the color or image. This is your body letting you know what colors or flowers you are excessive or deficient in.

Why Blend Color, Energy Medicine & Cannabis Essence?

Cannabis as a plant spirit supports the human system physically with our internal endocannabinoid system. Spiritually the Cannabis plant has been used to find a new consciousness or reality with its hallucinogenic compounds. As a cultivator plant, Cannabis has co-created a unique relationship with the human spirit. We have focused on the female plants as medicinal allies. We have worked with the genetics of this plant to highlight desired traits and remove traits that we dislike or that are not serving the cultivation of this plant. While we have focused on these aspects of the plant we have seen a relationship develop that is one so unlike any other relationship that humans have with plants. Therefore, the Cannabis/Human relationship is extremely unique. Factor in the intentions of this daily interaction to ascend spiritually and expand your heart consciousness! Can you sense the unlimited potential?

Primary & Complementary Colors

A complementary color is colors directly opposite each other in the color spectrum, such as red and green or blue and orange, that when combined in the right proportions, produce white light.
Primary Color: any of a group of colors from which all other colors can be obtained by mixing. This means that this is a foundational color. Example- Yellow and Blue = Green

VibroChromoTherapy Enhancement Card/Color Board

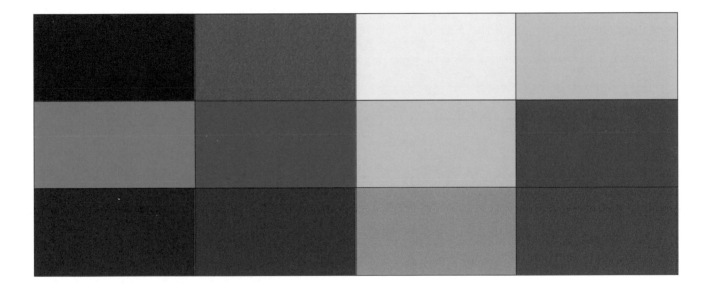

What are Color Boards?

The color boards are taking pure blocks of color and their complementary colors in the traditional color wheel and the CannaEssence[tm] color wheel. This creates a set of color therapy boards that work specifically with the vibration of the color and its accompanying flower essence. The colors were chosen from the Manchester color scale and testing for their standardization in a clinical setting.

You can use the color boards alone, with the CannaEssence™ or other vibrational remedies or tools like crystals or stones. These are extremely versatile as they work with the subconscious body-mind and the inner child through the body-mind connection.

I especially like to use them in my clinical practice in adjunct to our other work together. I find them to be excellent resources for the client as they can take them home and continue the body mind and reflection process that we started in the cannabis energy medicine or resonance session. This can take the healing to a much deeper, more fully resourced place where deep transformation can occur at the pace set by the client. I find this type of home or self-work serves only to make our sessions more potent as we can clearly work on issues as they are highlighted and being chinked on daily to let the inner layers shine their radiant light.

The boards are so easy to use that anyone can use them. Infants can nourish their energy systems through attraction and touch of the color to the skin as they play and go about their day. Just by the law of attraction, you will nourish your system by the color attraction that comes when you gaze at any of the color boards. If you leave them on a desk or hanging on a wall, they will infuse the space with balancing energy.

Cut & Play Color Boards at Back of Book

I have included in this book, a set of your very own core four master color boards at the end of the book. Is all you have to do is cut out your color boards and get to work & play ;) Use with the energetic hygiene exercises and other exercises in Part Two the Six Week Gide to Healing. I highly suggest you laminate your color boards after you cut them out to protect them and increase their resiliency.

LOOK FOR THESE LINES FOR CUTTABLES

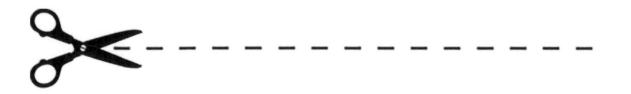

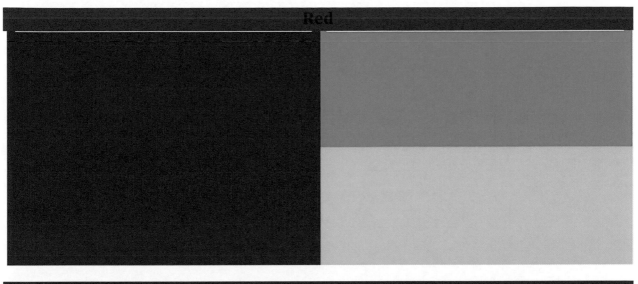

Red

RED in the positive: courage, pioneering, leadership qualities & drives, strong willed, confident, energetic, determined, and spontaneous, stimulating, energizing, love and joy for life, grounding, connected and grounded in physical body, inner knowing and connection to calling, stability, security

RED in the negative: fearful, fear of progress & change, ruthless, brutal, aggressive, anger, domineering, resentful, self-pitying, obstinate, quick-tempered, waring, lack of creativity, fight or flight, survival on a basic instinctual level, cold hands & feet, instability in physical body

Month: February – Month of grounding and breaking through stasis, self-awareness and your place on this planet, opening one's heart to possibilities through inner peace and stability

Day of the week: Tuesday

12 holy nights colors- 12 holy colors Date: December 26th

Planetary Association: Mars

Color Body Zone Association: Root Chakra – Base of Spine & tailbone

Organs: Kidneys, bladder, pelvis and hips, legs, vertebra, endocrine and adrenal glands and physical body in general

Traditional Complementary Color: Green

CannaEssence Complementary Color: Turquoise

Orange

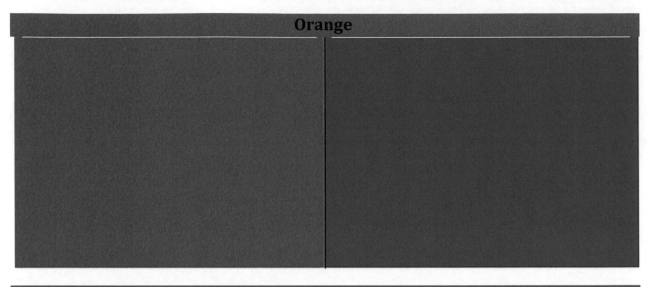

Color Association & Meanings - CHROMOTHERAPY indications: ORANGE

Orange in the positive: clear boundaries, clarity of self and other, responsibility for self, ability to see what is not yours, creativity, joyful, abundance, self-confidence, constructive, stimulating, energizing, warming, balancing environment, clarity of communication, emotions & intimacy

Orange in the negative: rigidity, isolation, despondency and despair, non-social, avoidance of others, PMS, menstrual complaints, IBS, testicular and prostate functional challenges, avoidance of color orange, aversion, resistance, excessive dehydration, GI & digestion, muscles & cramps

Month: March – month of profusion, abundance, joy & wealth

Day of the week: Thursday

12 holy nights colors- 12 holy colors Date: December 27th

Planetary Association: Jupiter

Color Body Zone Association: Pelvis, Sacrum

Organs: uterus, colon, prostate, ovaries, testes

Traditional Complementary Color: Blue

CannaEssence Complementary Color: Blue

Yellow

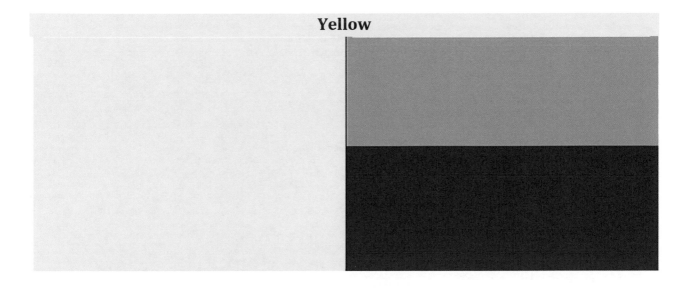

Yellow in the positive: Open minded, good-humored, confident, strategic, wise, logical, good-humored, intellectual, courageous, rebirth, rejuvenation, bright, joyful, increases neuromuscular tone, clearing-cleansing effect, mental clarity, inspiration, leadership, concentration, cleansing

Yellow in the negative: vindictive, looks for flattery, feelings of inferiority, over analytical, UTI, pessimistic, cowardly, devious, loss of hope, domination, chronic fatigue, low self-esteem

Month: April the month of rebirth from repetitive patterning and instability by balancing light in the body thus creating a healing relationship with the shadow of self

Day of the week: Wednesday

12 holy nights colors- 12 holy colors Date: December 28th

Planetary Association: Mercury (Messenger of the Gods)

Color Body Zone Association: Solar plexus

Organs: The endocrine system, pancreas, liver, spleen, stomach & small intestine

Traditional Complementary Color: Violet

CannaEssence Complementary Color: Indigo

Lime

Lime green in the positive: Deeply cleansing and purifying, blessings of light, objectivity in all situations, balanced detachment, open-hearted compassion & equanimity, Blessings from source, ascension, enlightenment, and awakening

Lime green in the negative: Feeling toxic, unclean, jealous, apathetic, lacking confidence, attached to outcomes, obsessive, overbearing, sensation of feeling stuck in the diaphragm or the abdomen on or near the ribs

Month: May – the month of rebirth and cleansing at every level you are ready and resourced enough to clear

Day of the week: Green day- use Friday

12 holy nights colors- 12 holy colors Date: December 29th

Planetary Association: Venus

Color Body Zone Association: Lower heart chakra right above the solar plexus and between the heart

Organs: diaphragm, stomach, mental

Traditional Complementary Color: Magenta

CannaEssence Complementary Color: Purple

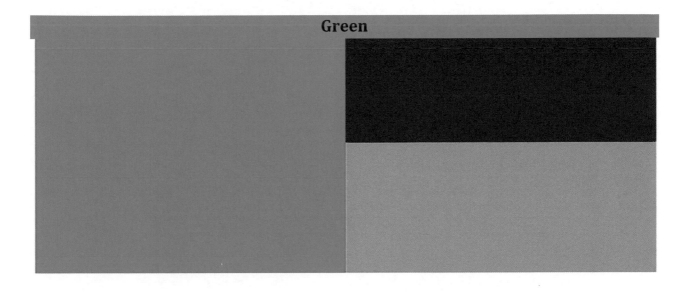

Green

Color Association & Meanings- CHROMOTHERAPY indications: **GREEN**

Green in the positive: deep self-love, generous, ability to give and take unconditionally, compassionate, harmonious, deeply connected to nature & living beings, adaptable, love children, deeply balancing as a neutral color between warm and cool, wholeness

Green in the negative: jealous, miserable, life revolving around possessions, indifferent or apathetic, unexplained heart and circulatory issues, autoimmune challenges, triggered by children or their noises i.e. laughter, no responsibility regarding money, trauma triggers

Month: June – open your heart month, moving non-serving or heated emotions with open heart centered communication and support from source – 2nd half of month

Day of the week: Friday

12 holy nights colors- 12 holy colors Date: December 30th AM

Planetary Association: Venus

Color Body Zone Association: Heart and chest center

Organs: heart, thymus, breasts

Traditional Complementary Color: Red

CannaEssence Complementary Color: Violet

Emerald

deep self-love, generous, ability to give and take unconditionally, compassionate, harmonious, deeply connected to nature & living beings, adaptable, love children, deeply balancing as a neutral color between warm and cool, wholeness

Green in the negative: jealous, miserable, life revolving around possessions, indifferent or apathetic, unexplained heart and circulatory issues, autoimmune challenges, triggered by children or their noises i.e. laughter, no responsibility regarding money, trauma triggers

Month: June – open your heart month, moving non-serving or heated emotions with open heart centered communication and support from source- First 2 weeks of the month

Day of the week: Friday

12 holy nights colors- 12 holy colors Date: December 30th PM

Planetary Association: Venus

Color Body Zone Association: Heart Center, chest

Organs: Heart, thymus, breast, Lymphatic deep flow

Traditional Complementary Color: Red

CannaEssence Complementary Color: Magenta

Turquoise

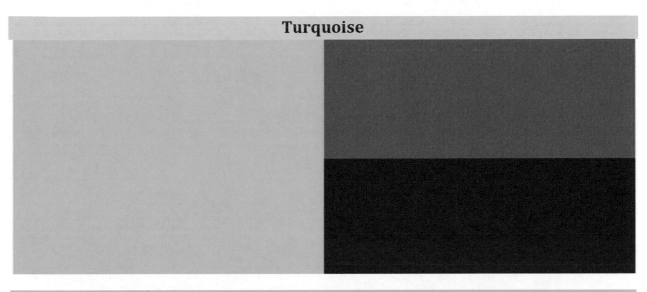

Color Association & Meanings- CHROMOTHERAPY indications: **TURQUOISE**

Turquoise in the positive: emotional healing, balancing, strengthening boundaries, strengthening immunity, radiates peace and tranquility, calming, restorative and gently invigorating, nervine to the nervous system, speech clarity and control, harmony, idealism

Turquoise in the negative: mental stress, tired, chronic fatigue, mental exhaustion, loneliness, lack of concentration, stress, immunity, and autoimmunity, scattered thinking, easily distracted, overly emotional, apathetic, lack of communication, unreliability, boastfulness, deception

Month: July – Strengthen your immune system month, clarify boundaries and remove obstacles to cure your immunity to life and speak your truth

Day of the week: N/A

12 holy nights colors- 12 holy colors Date: December 31st

Planetary Association: N/A

Color Body Zone Association: Thymus, Upper heart

Organs: thymus, immune system & lymphatic's, vocal cords

Traditional Complementary Colors: Orange

CannaEssence Complementary Color: Red

Blue

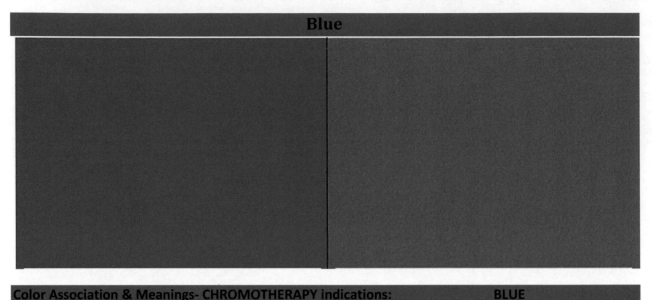

Color Association & Meanings- CHROMOTHERAPY indications:　　　　　**BLUE**

Blue in the positive: Clear self-expression and emotional responsibility in communication, Loyal, generous, trustworthy, peaceful, great mediators, truth, purposeful, synchronicity, truth, calming, relaxing and cooling

Blue in the negative: Cold, apathetic, non-trustworthy, disloyal, teeth and gum issues, TMJ, Fear of speaking, Inability to communicate thoughts into words, unsure of life purpose

Month: August- month of lungs, bringing in fresh oxygen to the tight or toned system that may be showing signs of overwork, pushing beyond one's owns limits

Day of the week: N/A

12 holy nights colors- 12 holy colors Date: January 1st

Planetary Association: N/A

Color Body Zone Association: Throat chakra, Upper heart

Organs: throat, lungs, endocrine and thyroid, upper GI

Traditional Complementary Color: Orange

CannaEssence Complementary Color: Orange

Indigo

Color Association & Meanings- CHROMOTHERAPY indications: **INDIGO**

Indigo in the positive: self-responsibility, trusting in one's soul path, highly intuitional, ability to see the whole not just my piece in it, Receiving intuitive messages as guidance, faithful, articulate, dutiful, fearless, sedating quality, divine knowledge

Indigo in the negative: fearful, intolerant, judgmental, easily depressed or despondent, tension headaches, ear and sinus challenges, inconsiderate of others, easily discouraged, feeling separated from others not just isolated but separated from source, lost

Month: September – balances the heart and mind on intention and mindfulness to manifest what you want

Day of the week: Saturday

12 holy nights colors- 12 holy colors Date: January 2nd

Planetary Association: Saturn

Color Body Zone Association: Third eye chakra in the middle of the forehead

Organs: Eyes, jaw, sinuses and pituitary gland

Traditional Complementary Color: Orange

CannaEssence Complementary Color: Yellow

Purple

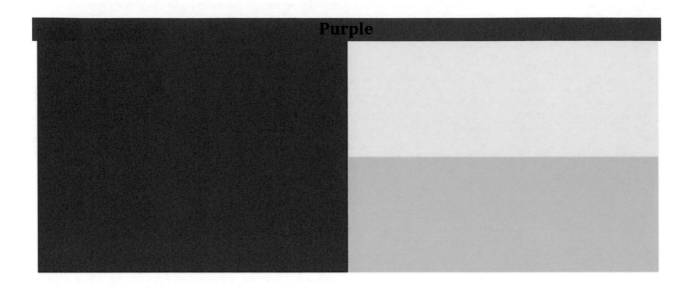

Color Association & Meanings- CHROMOTHERAPY indications: **PURPLE**

Purple in the positive: extremely transformative, contemplative, active red and passive blue work to balance the system, soft sensitive and highly intuitive, optimistic

Purple in the negative: Very serious, pessimistic or little hope for situation, outlook on life is dismal, dismisses intuition,

Month: November – a month of transformation from shock or trauma

Day of the week: Monday Am

12 holy nights colors- 12 holy colors Date: January 4th

Planetary Association: Moon

Color Body Zone Association: top of head, under armpits and lower posterior heart chakra

Organs: brain, head, pituitary

Traditional Complementary Color: Yellow

CannaEssence Complementary Color: Lime

Violet

Violet in the positive: self-knowledge and spiritual awareness, where a union of your higher self-blends with consciousness thus aligning the bioelectric field with source, calming and soothing effects like a balm on the soul, clarity of thought and action,

Violet in the negative: insomnia or other sleep disturbances, depression, mental disorders, dizziness or other equilibrium imbalances, fuzzy headedness, feeling superior to others, no concern for others, apathetic, unfeeling, fanaticism

Month: October – month of balance and rejuvenation from stress and tensions of the past year

Day of the week: Monday PM

12 holy nights colors- 12 holy colors Date: January 3rd

Planetary Association: Moon

Color Body Zone Association: crown chakra, head, brain

Organs: head, brain, pineal gland

Traditional Complementary Color: Yellow

CannaEssence Complementary Color: Green

Magenta

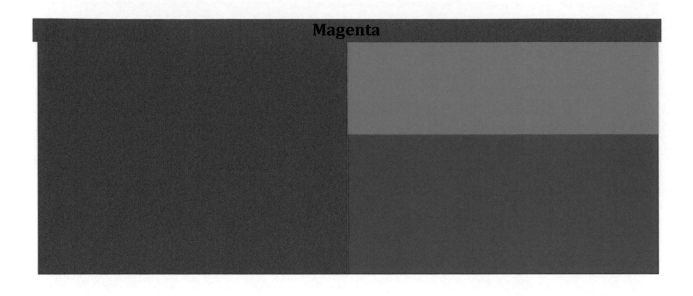

Color Association & Meanings- CHROMOTHERAPY indications: **MAGENTA**

Magenta in the positive: Self-validation, Agent of change, clearing old ways of thinking and doing that no longer serve the system, release past conditioning to create a new future

Magenta in the negative: Disassociated from self, stuck in old ways of thinking and being that no longer serve you, stuck in repetitive patterning, lack of energy to the bioelectric field, lack of stamina.

Month: December – month of actualization or birth into what you were manifesting

Day of the week: Sunday

12 holy nights colors- 12 holy colors Date: January 5th

Planetary Association: Sun

Color Body Zone Association: 8th chakra right above the head known as the soul star, back of the heart chakra- posterior

Organs: Heart, pineal and pituitary glands, adrenals

Traditional Complementary Color: Green

CannaEssence Complementary Color: Emerald

12 Colors Board

Part Two

6 Week Map
To
Self-Healing

Part two is the six-week map to self-healing using cannabis energy medicines. Each week you will work with one to three keys to health. Weekly you will build upon the foundation of self-healing from the previous week's Keys to Health. Every week has a focus on three keys to self-healing focusing on the weeks map or topic. I suggest you choose at least one key each week.

Part two was created as a map that can be used multiple times to raise your vitality and vibration. I like to pick and choose the Keys that support me where I am in that week. Some weeks I have more time and energy to apply all three keys, other weeks I will only be able to work with one. This is normal in self-healing and is part of the process of PEMS re-connection. Pick and choose from the week's keys to self-healing and you will be choosing the ones that support your PEMS right now.

I have laid out the keys to self-healing as a tool that can be used as three separate six week periods of self-healing. All level one keys are a perfect place for the beginner; level two are for the intermediate and level three for the advanced. If you are drawn toward mixing and matching the keys to your PEMS needs, then ignore this organizational suggestion. If you are feeling lost or overwhelmed start with level one for each week and then at the beginning of week seven start back at chapter six adding in level two keys for a six week period and so on with level three. By the eighteenth week, you will have a sense of which keys support your PEMS the most. While also being able to let go of and remove other keys that do not work with your life schedule, self-healing needs and intentions.

As you add keys to your life, you will find ones that fit easily into your life and others will not serve you as well. This is the natural order of finding the perfect tailored self-healing map to success. When you acknowledge that something does not work for you, you have eliminated a key that will not serve your self-healing process. This is excellent news and a clinical sign that you are well on your way to deep personal healing.

Every single one of you will experience some form of self-healing over the six week period if you use at least one key per week per day. Self-healing is not a quick pill that changes years of suffering in a blink of an eye. Self-healing takes time and vitality to elevate from a place of lower existence to one that is vibrating higher. Therefore, you can continue your great self-work over consecutive six-week journeys to self-healing. After all, every cell in our bodies is reborn every six weeks, why not maximize your keys to self-healing by writing a map for your cell rebirth or regencration.

Choose one key per section or choose them all according to your intention, imagery, and imagination.

"Healing is a matter of time, but it is sometimes also a matter of opportunity." – Hippocrates (460 BC-370 BC)

Chapter 6 **Week 1- Color Power**

In week one of your six-week map to self-healing you will be focusing on activating your color powers. Choose at least one key that you are drawn towards. During the week, I encourage you to embrace a more mindful approach to living in full color. This way you will start to notice what colors you are most attracted to and the colors that repel you. I encourage you to read about the colors that create an emotional or physical reaction. Read about its negative and positive qualities. Which ones have you been embracing? What is out of balance in your PEMS? Which color or colors will you work with first this week?

In Chapter five VibroChromoTherapy, you may have noticed that each color has a positive and negative expression in the PEMS system. Your goal is to activate the positive benefits of the twelve color rainbow using your natural gifts of color power.

In Chapter four, Cannabis Energy Medicine, the CannaEssence core four master flowers are co-created with a certain color, and they too have unique properties. This week serves as an opportunity to bring color into your life as a tool for healing and increased wellbeing using intention, imagination, and imagery. A easy way to find out is to look at the "what picture are you most attracted to" form below and in the resources section. You have seen this image in chapter four Cannabis Energy medicines, what color did you choose then? Is it the same one now?

*Free Download Link – What Flower are you most attracted to?

Key 1- Intuitive Eating – Eat by Color

The Intuitive Eating Approach

"The instinctual mind will never willingly move in the direction of deprivation, only toward greater nourishment"
Paul Bergner

Instinctively we all know what we each individually need for, our intuition guides us. In this modern era, it is difficult to feel or own our intuition all the time for it has been suppressed. However, you should be happy to know that it is always present all that you need to do to retrain yourself so that you may hear that "inner knowing" from within. Have faith, trust, and respect for your intuition; for it too translates into unconditional love for yourself, your body and your decisions. Once you can rebuild your relationship with yourself; you will clearly be able to hear your intuitive voice. In the meantime, work with these aspects along with your intuitive eating exercises. You may find that as you honor what your body is truly asking for.

Intuitive eating is a *process* of respecting your body and making peace with food—so that you are no longer bogged down with constant "food worry" thoughts. It's accepting that your health *and* your worth as a person do not change simply because you ate a so-called "bad" or "forbidden" food. This allows you to attain and, even more importantly, maintain a healthy weight and mentality that is natural for you.

Intuitive eating is based on a simple underlying premise: eat when you're hungry and stop when you're full. In other words, be able to say "yes" to food when "yes" is appropriate and to say "no" when "no" is appropriate. Intuitive eating is simple, but that doesn't mean it's easy for everyone. If you have a history of chronic dieting, rigid "healthy" rules about eating or don't like your body, it takes time and hard work. Why? Some things need to be in place, including the ability to trust yourself.

Intuitive Eating by Color Attraction

Intuitive eating by color attraction is a simple way of listening to your PEMS to activate your color and nutritional power using food. In Evelyn Tribole *Intuitive Eating book* she describes a ten-step process that works well. However it is emotionally messy. She asks that the reader takes a serious look at their food emotions and sensations in the body. For many people, if they do not have a clinician helping them through the process old patterns can emerge and can shake up the PEMS. I encourage a more simplified view of intuitive eating that rests in your empowered hands.

Eating by color attraction has some biological and psychological reasons for why we are attracted to certain foods or colors of foods. Biologically we crave the foods that contain the nutrients that our bodies need. Psychologically we are attracted to the colors that soothe our nervous system and support our current state of mind and health. Therefore, you will be attracted to the colors that will raise your vibration and nutrition via color attraction.

The below exercise encourages you to check in with your PEMS frequently and trust the guidance you are receiving when you activate your color power. Below is a description of the most common colors in the supermarket and their nutritional color powerhouse goodness.

Green vegetables & fruits contain lutein, an antioxidant that reinforces improved vision. Green supports cells, the lungs, and kidney health. Green foods contain potassium, vitamin c, vitamin k and folic acid. Some examples are broccoli, green beans, bell peppers, lettuces, kale and other greens.

Orange/Yellow colored vegetables and fruits are rich in beta carotene and vitamin c. They help promote the excellent vision, healthy skin, healthy growth & development and supports a strong immune system. Some examples are oranges, butternut squash, winter squash, carrots.

Red colored vegetables and fruits are rich in phytochemicals like lycopene and anthocyanins. Which improve heart health, prostate health and diminish the risk of cancer through DNA health. Some examples are peppers, tomatoes, apples.

Purple/ Blue fruits and vegetables are rich in antioxidants and phytochemicals that are anti-aging and reduce the risk of cancer and support mental clarity.

White fruits and vegetables are rich in phytochemicals and potassium. They help reduce cholesterol levels, lower blood pressure and prevent diabetes. Some examples are, mushrooms, onions, radishes.

How to Intuitive Eating

The easiest way to start this is to go to a grocery store or farmers market where you can see all the vegetables and fruits laid out in front of you.

1. Take a moment to do a body check and see what is going on with your PEMS.
   a. If you have pain or discomfort, note it on your mental inventory.
2. When you are done with your body check look up at all the food in front of you.
3. Ask your PEMS what one color will nourish you the most.
4. Once you have a color in mind, head over to the section with that color that is shining most brightly at you.
5. When you are in front of the color let your PEMS choose, take a close look at each of the fruits or vegetables in that area. Which one are you most attracted to?
6. Choose one piece of fruit or a vegetable and pick it up in your hands.
7. Ask your PEMS if this food will nourish it deeply and encourage self-healing
   a. If the answer is yes- place it in your basket and eat up
   b. If the answer is no- place the food back and start back at #1
8. Once you have chosen the color or colors that are most nutritious for your PEMS take a look below and see what your body may be missing nutritionally.
9. You can repeat the process or continue your shopping starting at #1 until you are doing this automatically.

Key 2- Choose Your Clothes by Color

In key number two, I want to encourage you to be more mindful about your color choices in your everyday life. Just like in key one, where you start to be aware of the foods you are eating and the colors that you are most attracted to, you will expand this concept to your clothes and adornments like jewelry. Being mindful of your color attraction daily is a type of mindfulness re-patterning that breaks old habits and encourages higher frequency patterning. When you choose a color it is helpful to read about your color choice in chapter five VCT. By doing this choosing of color and mindful reflection, you will highlight your shadow pack and make long lasting changes to your PEMS. This can create beautiful results like self-healing. By re-connecting your PEMS through color and picture attraction, you can change the way you interact with the world.

How to Clothes by Color Attraction

1. Do a body check
    a. Sense what is going on in your PEMS-
    b. Create a mental inventory
2. Ask your PEMS what one color would support you the most.
3. Then imagine yourself wearing this color from your wardrobe.
    a. You may be wearing all this color, an article of clothing or just a piece of jewelry or adornment. Let your imagination out to play
4. Review the color you choose in Chapter five for reflection & mindfulness
    a. Is there something in your life that needs this support right now?
    b. Use your color attraction to support you when you need it the most
        i. Increase your vibration & those around you
5. You can choose up to three colors per day with this focused reflection

Key 3- Color Boards Daily Practices & Exercises

Energetic hygiene is very important for all life forms. Have you ever watched a cat clean itself with intent and ferocity and do it frequently? Yes, they do like to be clean physically, but the act of mindfully (using the tongue their sensory organ) cleaning the body acts very similarly to the way some folks use brushing energetically and physically to discard unwanted or non-serving energy and dead skin cells. Think of the difference in feeling and sensing a nice hot soapy shower vs. brushing with hands or brushing with a bristled brush. All three have a different energetic quality as well as application to the body. These are similar concepts of cleanliness and movement.

A soapy hot bath has water that is smooth and flowing with heat. The heat is drawing and moving things away with the help of the slippery suds cleaning the area making it squeaky clean. The hand brushing is brisk, flowing and being created by your movements, depth, speed and intention. Are you slow and methodical? Brisk and flowing with throwing motions etc.? Then the traditional dry brush skin brushing that can be dry or mixed with oils. In this example, we will discuss the dry brushing. A tolerable bristled brush is used to invigorate, move and shake dead skin cells off. In each instance, a different energetic result will occur, so these are seemingly different; however in the energetic hygiene realm, they are just different forms of application to achieve the same ends. The preference comes from the user which will be dependent upon the constitution, energetic needs, background and so forth.

Personally, I have 5-6 different ways of doing daily energetic and physical clearing that work well for my system at different times of the year, day and my mood or pain levels. My favorite is to use color boards or geometric shape boards to place them intuitively around me in a circle and then place any essences, rocks, or other resources on the boards while I suck up all the goodness from the middle. I have received treatments with a practitioner performing the energetic clearing and shifting by their intuition, and it was just as potent with a more resourced quality. That therapeutic net is awesome!

Energetic Hygiene with the Color Circuit

Exercise #1- Core 4 - Bioelectric circle circuit boards

1. Perform the body check

2. Take all four of your CannaEssence color boards in your hands *(cut out from the back of the book)*

    a. Intuitively start placing the boards around you in a circle

    b. You may omit or use all the boards according to your inner guidance

    c. *If you are having trouble sensing what to do- just start placing the boards around you from the top to the bottom around you in a circle*

3. *Optional-* Use Core Four CannaEssence Master Flower bottles. Then take any essences that call to you by your attraction to them. Place them on the boards in any configuration you like

    a. You may then be drawn towards taking an essence internally or putting it on your body

        i. Take the essence 3-6 drops internally, or apply externally according to your bodies needs

    b. You may also be drawn towards putting a drop or two of the essence on one of the color boards. This is a way to receive the vibrations through the resonancy field without having to take the essence internally. Lamination required first.

4. At this point, you may feel as if you are done or the work is complete. You can close the session with a bow to the essences, and colors that came to your aid in your work for the day

5. Then, I usually step out of the circle and see if my system wants to do anything outside of the circle

    a. Do I want to move the boards around and get in there again?

    b. Do I want to take some out and work with only a few? You can then repeat the above process until you feel complete

6. ***Closing Options:***

a. Once I feel complete, I tend to do a smudge of Palo Santo to fill in any missing gaps, holes or wisps in my bioelectric field

b. If I'm in a place where the scent is not serving, I will *use my intention to fill* in any gaps and holes in my field with whatever will serve me to my highest and greatest good. At first, it may seem like you are just having faith in this filling in quality. After practice, you will be able to sense the changes happening to your system. Use the body check before and after to help guide the process of trusting your senses. A journal can be helpful for those walking the journey of reconnection with their body

Exercise #2- VCT – 12 Color Bioelectric circle circuit boards

1. Perform the body check

2. Take all twelve of the VibroChromoTherapy color boards in your hands *(cut out from the back of the book)*

   a. Intuitively start placing the twelve boards around you in a circle

   b. You may omit or use all the boards according to your inner guidance

   c. *If you are having trouble sensing what to do- just start placing the boards around you from the top to the bottom around you in a circle*

3. If you are being called to move your body

   a. Gently spin and rotate in the circle allowing your body to move as it wants to

4. If you would like to meditate or contemplate the colors and images, sit down in the circle

   a. Soft gaze focuses on the images or color boards as your focus point for this meditation session

   b. Choose one image from the twelve color boards around you. Pick the chosen color up in your hand. Use a focus point for your meditation.

5. At this point, you may feel as if you are done or the work is complete. You can close the session with a bow to the colors that came to your aid in your work for the day if you are called.

6. Then, I usually step out of the circle and see if my system wants to do anything outside of the circle

a. Do I want to move the boards around and get in there again?

b. Do I want to take some out and work with only a few? You can then repeat the above process until you feel complete

7. ***Closing Options:***

a. Once I feel complete, I tend to do a smudge of Palo Santo to fill in any missing gaps, holes or wisps in my bioelectric field

b. If I'm in a place where the scent is not serving, I will *use my intention to fill* in any gaps and holes in my field with whatever will serve me to my highest and greatest good. At first, it may seem like you are just having faith in this filling in quality. After practice, you will be able to sense the changes happening to your system. Use the body check before and after to help guide the process of trusting your senses. A journal can be helpful for those walking the journey of reconnection with their body

Exercise #3- Bioelectric VibroChromoThearapy™ Broadcast

The bioelectric VibroChormoTherapy broadcast is a great way to do energetic hygiene while you are in an environment or space. I particularly like to use color boards to infuse my workspace.

1. Perform the body check

2. Choose the most attractive color to you at this moment

3. Then take the color board, color card or essence and place it in the space you will be working with the intention that this nourish you will all the qualities that your system was asking for

   a. *If in an environment with lots of folks- make sure to*

focus your broadcast to ONLY you. Please be respectful of others unique paths and ways of being

4. Optional- You can tailor it to your needs by adding water bowl broadcasts with essences or on top of the color boards or CannaEssence images

   b. Let simplicity out to play

5. Change when your system is no longer attracted to that particular image, color or color board

Chapter 7 Week 2- Present Power

The being present superpower is a present to yourself. It is full of long lasting benefits that serve as a foundation for all your other work in future weeks. By embracing the present power, you will be able to create long lasting changes for your PEMS systems. Being present in the face of chaos and turmoil can be a difficult task for any conscious soul. Do not give up, keep working at it and engage with your discomfort for being in the present moment.

For many people with chronic conditions or illness, they are looking for ways to self-heal. These folks tend to have old habits of survival that worked to separate oneself from their body so that they could continue. Now as you are healing and reconnecting the PEMS this old patterning is no longer serving. It is time to transform the avoidance factor and embrace the discomfort. As you work more with your discomfort of being in the present moment, the activation will decrease and the present moment will truly feel like a gift. This process is not overnight, more often than not it can take time and much focus to find the gift on the other side. My suggestion is to be gentle with yourself, letting your present super power unfurl in its own time.

As you become more comfortable with being in the present moment, these keys will seem like a much smaller mountain to tackle. Slow and steady. If you are having resistance to these exercises, give yourself an ok button to have these sensations and feelings. Chose bite size chunks to work with until you are more mindful and present. For most people, the sense that these exercises are easy or simple will show that you can go deeper and balance that which was once imbalanced.

Key 1- Intuitive Eating – Eat with Mindfulness

Week two is a continuation of the intuitive color powered eating that you started in week one. This week your focus is not on color but on the food itself and all the sensory experiences that come along with mindful eating. Just like a great food critic or a wine critic these people have brought their senses directly into the present to experience the food fully with all of the PEMS and the five senses. Mindful eating can take a little bit of practice and may serve as a foundational key for all other weeks as well.

Mindful Sensory Eating

The best way to start to work with mindful eating is to slow down the speed at which you chew and swallow your food. By slowing down and coming into the present, you can sense the texture of the food. Notice the temperature, flavor, and taste as you slowly chew. What do you enjoy or dislike about the food you are eating? Was it enhanced or depleted by your present power? What words or image would you use to describe the food?

Mindful Food Imagination

Exercise to image where your food came from, how far it had to travel to get to you will open up a whole new sensory experience. If your food is local it may not have had a long distance to travel. However if you're eating an avocado from Mexico, it had to come a long way to get where you are. The easiest way to active your presence power with mindful food imagination is to conjure up the image of the food in your mind's eye. I have shared below my musing about the avocado. Explore your imagination, imagery and intention this week with presence power.

For example, imagine an avocado hanging on a tree in the heat. A group of farm workers get in harnesses and climb the tree, gently cutting the stalk and releasing the fruit. They are dipped in a cold bucket of water to cool the fruit before processing and get rid of any pollens that can not cross international lines. The avocado gets packages, placed on a truck, then on a plane, then another truck until it gets to my supermarket. I then choose this special and unique avocado through intuitive color power eating and now it is in my chicken salad. Now its life is going to nourish my life, by increasing my vibration and nutritional status.

Key 2- Mindfulness in Daily Tasks

Key two is all about deepening your relationship to your PEMS present powers. After experiencing heightened sensory experiences with food you are ready to engage with more mindfulness in your daily life.

Start with the Toothbrush

The best way to start to bridge the gap between mindful eating and mindful daily tasks is to take a task you do at least two times a day and work with it for six-week timeframes. Every day as you brush your teeth you want to bring in your mindfulness techniques learned in key one of week two. Every time you brush your teeth sense into the feel of the brush against your teeth, lips, gums, tongue. Is the sensation the same on each region? What is the difference?

As you continue to sense your PEMS in reaction to your toothbrush you can start to cultivate this mindfulness into other tasks or activities. In this way, you can gain control over your mind and the reactions of the PEMS when you are in a place of presence.

Key 3- PEMS Protection Power

Your PEMS protection power comes from mindful PEMS awareness and is used to protect you from outside influences. The PEMS protection power is very much like a shield that cocoons you as you transform and change into the butterfly you are. As a sensitive person, I needed to active my PEMS protection power daily during my self- healing path. I use its protection daily as a way to navigate the world with confidence and grace. I hope to encourage you to imagine your bubble of protection when you need it. Draw from it the strength that you need to support your PEMS in times of stress and discomfort. The bubble of protection will serve you well as you grow and expand your PEMS consciousness.

With this key, the magic of PEMS protection comes from your imagery, imagination, and intention. Let those be the limiting factor to the power you possess.

Chapter 8 **Week 3- PEMS Power**

In week three you will be activating your PEMS power to another degree. As you have been working with the PEMS by way of the general body check in your mind's eye, you will be invited this week to engage in journaling your PEMS changes before you choose your tools of support. This is one of the weeks that you will most likely need to engage in two keys to get the full benefit of the self-healing experience. Remember if you are not challenging yourself to raise your vibration you are not growing and self-healing. Continue to re-connect to your PEMS and find your PEMS power activated.

Key 1- Body Check Journal Form

This week with your body check we will go deeper into your self- evaluations to deepen the body- mind connection. This is a continuation from previous weeks just as much as it is the foundation for all the other work you will be doing with yourself. In fact, I would say that this is the most important week due to this foundational quality. I have included a form in this chapter as well as another one to copy and re-use at the end of the book in the resources section. I encourage you to fill out a journal form at least three times this week, to ingrain the action of self-reflection and intention into your daily life. Get good at self-evaluation and your PEMS will let you know where to go for your next great step to self-healing.

 *Free Download Link –Personal Journal Form

You can use this form with any Cannabis Energy Medicine Technique or VibroChromoTherapy techniques you have learned in this book. Please use it as an opportunity to deepen your relationship with yourself so that the path to self-healing is paved in PEMS power.

CannaEssence **Personal Journal Form for the Core 4**

Name: _____ Date: _____

1. **Are you currently experiencing any of the following?**

   Pain/tenderness ❏ No ❏ Yes: Stress ❏ No ❏ Yes: Allergies ❏ No ❏ Yes   Anxiety, Fear, Depression ❏ No ❏ Yes

   Numbness/tingling ❏ No ❏ Yes: Stiffness ❏ No ❏ Yes: Recent surgery ❏ No ❏ Yes: Swelling ❏ No ❏ Yes

   Mental suffering ❏ No ❏ Yes: Emotional imbalance ❏ No ❏ Yes: New Consciousness ❏ No ❏ Yes

2. **Which color or colors Are you working with today?** *Circle one below*

   Red_____   Green   Purple   Violet

3. **Perform a body check before you use the essences or color boards. What do you notice in your PEMS? Please note any physical, emotional, mental or spiritual imbalances you are experiencing in the space & body below:**

Before

Burning	Tightness or discomfort	Ache	Sharp Pain	Numbness	Other	Aura/field Holes
======	oooooooooo	xxxx	//////////	*****	zzzzz	*You Fill in with colors or drawing*

4. **Choose an essence or application method & make sure to give those areas that came up in #3 a little more attention.**

5. **After your personal session, perform another body check and notice what has shifted and what still is asking for attention.**

Where Did You Apply During the Session

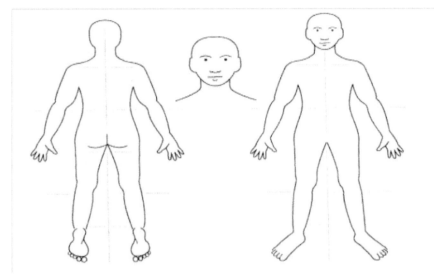

After

Burning	Tightness or discomfort	Ache	Sharp Pain	Numbness	Other	Aura/field Holes
=====	ooooooooooo	xxxx	//////////	*****	zzzzz	*You Fill in with colors or drawing*

Key 2- Aura & Auric Infusions

Aura infusing is supportive when other treatments are contraindicated or the person is unable to take the essences internally or externally for some reason. This could be due to PEMS sensitivity, skin infections, rashes, irritation or pregnancy. I especially like to use auric infusions for daily energetic hygiene as my system is very sensitive and cannot always take the essences of my physical body every day. I have included a section, especially for pregnancy and baby.

Auric infusions are excellent for a frail or convalescing system and can add energy, a cushion or protective cocoon around the energy bodies. I have seen this to be especially useful after the skin has been physically invaded by some object whether that's taking blood or drugs via syringe, surgery, a physical blow or drugs that change cell function. As we discussed in the section on auras when the bioelectric field is invaded in some way we can see holes, gaps, wisps and other malfunctions occurring. By using the auric infusions your system with being more able to communicate with your inner physician through your attraction to a certain bottle or color.

If you listen to your body closely, it will tell you everything you need to know to proceed with your inner healing journey. *If you have challenges with sensing what cues your body is giving you. I suggest using Green for at least 1-3 months until you can trust in the information you are receiving. By taking Green it connects you directly to your body, allowing the body to reconnect to the entire PEMS so that all centers can communicate in fluidic ease just like a superconductive highway. Then for the same amount of time you can work with Violet to mop up anything that was shaken loose by the reconnect of the PEMS.*

In pregnancy, auric infusions are an excellent application method as it can be very gentle or powerful depending on your intention. If the mom is very sensitive, I highly suggest starting with this method before exploring any of the others. The use of flower essences during pregnancy has been seen as safe for there are no active ingredients that could cause an allergic reaction or changes in the moms' blood chemistry. However, due to the nature of flower essences, they naturally work with the shadows of ourselves they can shake up stuff that we thought was long and gone. Some flower essence practitioners feel that the essences can interact with the soul expression of the baby as the mom is a pristine vessel that is free from her karmic baggage as she births this new being with its karmic baggage. In my practice I let the mom and the baby be the ones who make the choices about which essences are used and which are not. The mom and baby start an inner dialogue that builds trust within the womb so that by birth the relationship is held by a foundation of respect, active listening and acceptance of self-expression through true equanimity.

Color Board Auric Infusion Directions:

Perform the body check and get a sense of what is going on in your body. Then take your stack of color boards and place them around you in a circle on the floor. These do not have to be in any particular order. It is best to place them intuitively around yourself as you do in the daily hygienic exercises. If you have placed one color board in the middle of the circle, this is the board you will use to perform the auric infusion. If you have not placed a board in the middle, it is time to step into the middle of the circle and find the one color board to work with at this moment. Let your eyes begin to go out of focus a bit gazing at the color boards on the ground. Then start turning slowly 360 degrees looking for the one color board that is brighter than the others, calling your attention repeatedly back, or that you see that color in every color board you notice. These are your cues that that is the one color board to auric infuse for the day. Grab all the other color boards placing them in a stack to the side. Then take the chosen color board and find a comfortable place to sit or stand according to your PEMS needs and your personal preferences. Turn the color board facing you within two into 24 inches depending on your arm length and where you are sensing the PEMS needs support. You may be called to move the board over certain areas of the body as well as moving it within your entire PEMS system. With your intention start to broadcast the colors from the color squares on your color board. With your mind's eye, imagine the colors raying out of the board letting the colors seep into your PEMS. Filling the room with color on your color board. Breathe them into any areas of discomfort. Continue to breathe in the colors and move the board anywhere that you are drawn. After a time your system will feel done. You may be drawn to opening your eyes with a sense of completion. Perform the body check again and notice what sensations have shifted. Close. Cleanup.

Direct Aura Infusion using bottles – OPTIONAL Directions:

Perform the body check and get a sense of what is going on in your body. Then take a look at your CannaEssence set asking which essence will serve you most today. Pick the bottle up and put 1-2 drops of an elixir into the palms of your hands, making sure not to touch the dropper to your skin. Rub your palms together gently. Take 1 -2 deep breaths allowing your body to soak up the color and essence through your palms. Allow your hands to float up to your chest, palms facing towards your heart. Encourage the essence to seep into your auric fields, nourishing them with your chosen essence of the day. Let your hands be guided to a different location on your body or in your field. You may be called to stand up, sit down or move around. Allow movement to occur without judgment or need to know why you're doing what you're doing. When you sense that, your PEMS is fully saturated, place the color board on the ground in front of you and perform another body check. This time being away from any changes that have happened since your starting inventory. Are there any areas that are still calling for attention? Would the PEMS like the same color or picture you were working with before? Or Does the system want another color? If the system would like another color, start back at the beginning doing quick body checks so that another bottle color or picture choice arises. Do this until the PEMS system no longer wants any more colors or pictures. Perform a body check and notice what sensations have shifted. Close. Cleanup.

Direct Aura Infusions for Pregnancy Directions:

Moms may want to add in a baby body check during the body check exercise. Then see which essence baby wants and which mom wants. Sometimes, moms need to do two infusions; one for mom and one for baby. Moms, please be mindful when you do the body check and have conflicting messages from your body and the babies. For Example, you want and desperately need violet, but the baby says no. This is when an inner dialogue between mother and child can occur even when in the womb. If you acknowledge that no and ask what support if any the baby needs the answer may change, but it may stay as a resounding no. It is your job to stay unattached to the answer and allow what needs to be supported rise to the surface. If you have a name for the child, please use this when referring to the baby.

Perform the body check exercise and get a sense of what is going on in your body. Then take a look at your CannaEssence set asking which essence will serve you most today? Pick the bottle up and touch it to your heart acknowledging your needs. Then place the bottle back in line with the essences. Place your hand over the baby or with your intention become aware of baby PEMS and ask what one essence will support baby most today? Pick the bottle that lights up or seems almost too easy. If it feels hard, forceful, or silent. STOP. Tap into the baby. Do a BABY body check and ask the question again? Which one essence will serve BABY most today? Open each bottle and put 1-2 drops of each elixir into one palm. Close the bottle top with the free hand. Make sure not to touch the dropper to your skin. Rub your palms together gently. Take 1-2 deep breaths allowing your body to soak up the color/s and essence/s through your palms. Allow your hands to float up to your chest, palms facing towards your heart. Encourage the essence to seep into your auric fields, nourishing them with your chosen essence of the day. Let your hands be guided to spots in your PEMS. You may be called to stand up, sit down or move around. Allow movement to occur without judgment or need to know why you're doing what you're doing. Let the system absorb as much of the essence as it needs. When the system has had enough, you will notice a desire to get up and go about your day, or you may be drawn towards another CannaEssence bottle. If that is the case, you will start from the beginning continuing until you are no longer attracted to a certain color or picture where the whole line up of bottles just looks pretty, and you see it as a whole instead of one standing out more than the others. Perform a body check and notice what sensations have shifted. Close. Cleanup.

Baby Body Check Exercise Directions:

Perform the body check for your system mom before checking into the baby. Once you have a sense of what is going on in your PEMS systems, it is time to check into a baby. *Get in a comfortable position with your hands resting on your belly. With your minds eye sink into your skin…through the muscular layers and the womb. You will sense the distinctly different energy quality of the being within you. Take the baby in as a whole, sensing everything from the toes to the head. Encourage a vision of baby to appear in your mind's eye....sensing what the baby's PEMS is trying to communicate. Breath awareness into a baby is starting at the feet with two deep breaths, letting the area fall away like leaves on the second exhale. Continue up the body with the legs, torso, arms & hands, neck & head all the while washing over the baby with mindful awareness. Take the baby in as a whole and notice if anything has shifted or is calling for more attention. When the system is complete and content gently withdrawal your awareness and come back into your body. Do a quick personal inventory. What has shifted in your body check since checking in with the baby? Are there any areas that would like some additional attention or awareness? Close & Cleanup.*

Key 3- Color Infusions with an Energy Partner

1. *Simple Color Board Infusion with Energy Partner Directions:*

Using color boards with an energy partner is an excellent resource for daily hygienic aura cleansing as well as a boatload of fun. ☺ This is a great way to cultivate the skills needed to work with deeply with yourself in a health-oriented capacity. Make sure to do this exercise with a chair that you can easily walk around and reach most of your energy partner's body. A high back kitchen chair works nicely as well as a folding chair or an exercise ball.

Perform the body check and get a sense of what is going on in each of your bodies before you start this exercise. Designate who will be the one GIVING & the one RECEIVING first. The receiver can keep eyes closed, open or in a soft gaze, whatever is most comfortable and gets them connected to their PEMS. *Giver stands up in front of the receiver. Take the color board deck and wash your awareness over your energy partner. Performing a PEMS body check with your intuition. Notice any areas that are calling for attention and note them so you can serve them in a moment. Then start to walk around your energy partner placing color boards on the floor surrounding the chair using your intuition. Once you have placed the boards that will serve your partner you can discard any unused boards by placing them face down on the side. Then return standing in front of your energy partner. Use your intention and mind's eye to activate the color boards broadcasting their color into the receiver. Encourage the color boards to grow in intensity as they surround and infuse the persons PEMS in front of you. Perform a verbal & intuitional body check and notice what sensations have shifted. Close. Cleanup.*

Chapter 9 **Week 4- Flower Power**

In week four you will be working with flower power basics as you continue through your six-week healing plan. Each week you will engage more fully with your inner flower powers through your intelligent waters. You can use the core four master flower color boards at the back of the book as a short-term replacement for the essences in any of the following keys. Know that the quantum infusion method is not as powerful or vibrationally pure as the quick Cannabis Energy Medicine Making technique below. After a time the quantum infusion technique will be too low a vibration for your PEMS, and you will need the pure, elevated vibration of the CannaEssences themselves. However, until that time comes you are well prepared to self-heal with all the tools in this book.

NOTE- if you do not have the CannaEssences to work with. You can use the Quantum infusion technique as a replacement for the essences see below. Then use in the preparations below.

1. ***Quantum Infused Intelligent Water– Use within 12 Hours***

    Use your core four color boards at the back of the book to make activated intelligent water using your CannaEssence color board. Is all you will need is a small glass of water. You can then use this in replacement of drops of essence below. A quantum infusion is less powerful than the actual essence. However, it will be of some use as you activate your intention, imagination, and imagery towards your final goals of self-healing and elevating your environment.

Perform a personal body check to get a sense of the PEMS and its needs today at this moment. With the core four master flower color boards in hands with eyes closed or soft gaze, ask what one color will support you most and then open your eyes and gaze at your color boards. Does one color or picture stand out from the rest? Perhaps it looks brighter than the others, or your eye is just drawn back towards that one image. Place your small glass of water on top of the chosen image for at least 20 minutes to allow your intelligent water to infuse. Use within twelve hours. For every drop of essence that the recipe calls for you will use one teaspoon of the prepared and activated waters.

Key 1- Drops of Flowers

Most flower essence books are written around the imbalances seen in a person and the benefits of the essence of the human or animal using them. The simplicity of color or picture attraction is your true indicator, and this is why the CannaEssence system is so unique. Due to this exceptional quality, we had to develop other ways of working with the essences as human consciousness shifts our physical, emotional, mental and spiritual bodies. In my experience, the increased sensitivity is the biggest challenge to working with the essences. There are so many people who are affected by the essences in such a dramatic way that more sensitivity calibration is needed to balance the system. Therefore, the below options were birthed to serve each who will use the CannaEssences.

I suggest that you work on your system to find your preferred application method. Start with the application that you are most attracted to or curious about. Perform the application and see how your system reacts to that particular application. It is important to note that if you try a stronger application and react strongly if you try a more subtle or gentle method, you most likely will find your perfect application through this self-exploration process. Also, your system may react differently when the vitality is low verse when it is fully nourished and thriving. Do not worry about being right or knowing exactly what you are doing. Allow yourself the opportunity to take part of the inner journey to listen, sense and act on the information that you receive from yourself work. This may look different for each person, so please allow yourself some space to see what will serve your system the most. Sometimes I need the dosage bottle; other times I need auric infusions, only the color boards, a spritz or a bath. Allow your body and your attraction to guide you or affirm your intuitional messages or subtle cues. Simplicity = Easy button to the PEMS.

Traditional Flower Essence Use and Application

Most flower essences are taken internally at four drops four times a day for one lunar cycle or 30 days. For the purpose of this six-week self-healing program, you will want to take your chosen essence for at least one week to get the most benefit. You can continue to take the essences internally they are usually diluted from the stock bottle. You can make your dosage bottle taking one drop of the essence from your CannaEssence bottle and mixing it with water in a ½ oz Boston round dropper bottle. Dosage bottles are very handy to put in your pocket or purse. By creating a dosage bottle, you protect the longevity and purity of your stock bottle. My favorite use of a dosage bottle is for someone who needs prolonged exposure to the essence or for those who are very sensitive to the essences. Those who would need to use the essences for an extended period would be folks who have long-standing imbalances that the remedy supports. Students of self-work especially love to study the essence and its effects on the system over the course of a month. A dosage bottle is also a great place to start when you are new to the essences. We encourage those who are new to the essences to choose their favorite color and work with that for the course of a month.

A Dosage bottle is a great place to start!

How to Make a Dosage Bottle Using Color Boards:
How to prepare your dosage bottle using color boards:

1. Fill your dosage bottle with spring water
   a. You may add a few drops of brandy or your favorite cordial for a deeper preservative effect. Good if you will be touching the dropper to your tongue- OPTIONAL
2. Then choose the color or essence you want to work with for the month
3. Place your dosage bottle on top of the chosen picture or color. Let sit for 24 hours.
4. You are now prepared to use your dosage bottle (see direction below)

How to Use Your Dosage Bottle: Choose 1 of the below methods to work with your dosage bottle.

1. *Set Dosage frequency:* Take four drops 4x a day by mouth for one lunar cycle or 6 weeks if you are doing a protocol
2. *Intuitional & body talk method of dosing:*

a. Keep the essence in your pocket & take it whenever you think about it

How to Make a Dosage Bottle Using Essences:
How to prepare your dosage bottle:

1. Fill your dosage bottle with spring water
2. You may add a few drops of brandy or your favorite cordial for a deeper preservative effect. Good if you will be touching the dropper to your tongue- OPTIONAL
3. Then choose your essence to work with for the month
4. Add one drop of the desired essence to the brown dropper bottle
5. You are now prepared to use your dosage bottle (see direction below)

How to Use Your Dosage Bottle: Choose 1 of the below methods to work with your dosage bottle.

5. *Set Dosage frequency:* Take four drops 4x a day for one lunar cycle or 6 weeks if you are doing a protocol
6. *Intuitional & body talk method of dosing:*
   a. Keep the essence in your pocket & take it whenever you think about it

Key 2- Flower Water Self Treatment

Cotton ball applications are a fantastic tool for self-care or in a session atmosphere. This is an especially useful method for those who have sensitive constitutions as you can choose the timeframe that the essence is on the skin. The cotton ball method is the most diverse application in our tool belts as you can apply the essences anywhere on the body. The cotton ball method is my preference when working with myself or my clients as it can easily be converted into a long-term application or compress. By using this method, it can decrease the amount of transference and absorption of client energy. The cotton ball application is excellent for compressing wide body zones, direct acupoints or full spine applications.

Basic Treatment Cup Preparation Directions:

The cotton ball method is excellent for sensitive constitutions or direct point or body zone applications. Cotton ball applications are perfect for applying to anywhere on the body. It is my preferred method when working with clients. It helps with less transference & absorption of energy using this method. It is excellent for compressing, acupoint or chakra point or spine applications.

Perform a body check. Choose the essence to apply to your PEMS. Fill your treatment cup or bowl with warm to hot water. Add 1-6 drops of the chosen essence. Dip a cotton ball or cotton pad into the treatment cup or small bowl of water. Gently squeeze from the top so that you are not dripping essence. Then *apply to body zones of pain or discomfort that came up in the body check exercise* using the short term or long term options below. Once you apply the essence to the body, I invite you to, *go lay down or get horizontal for 45 minutes or so.* This will allow the PEMS to integrate all the changes and rise to a higher level of being. After you have taken some integration time, *perform another body check. What has shifted? Changed? Needs more attention?*

1. **Option 1- Local Short-Term Application**: You can choose just to rub the liquid over the area and throw the application pad into the garbage or compost.

2. **Option 2- Compress Long Term Application:** You can choose to apply the essence to the area for an extended period. This would allow you to use it to compress or pain vacuum an area.

How to: Use Application Pads & Cotton Balls:
Directions:

1. Fill your treatment cup with warm to hot water
2. Add 3-6 drops of the essence
3. Apply to body zones of pain or discomfort that came up in the body check exercise. Use it to compress or pain vacuum.
4. Or Apply to the spine by dipping the cotton ball into the bowl of water and placing the cotton ball at the top of spine and squeeze. Allow the liquid to trail down the spine and either soak into your clothes or underwear line for long term compression or when unclothed allow the essence to soak into the body. Air drying.
5. You can go lay down horizontal for at least 45 minutes OR
6. You can go about your day
7. Body check to see what shifts have occurred

How to Make a Compress:
Directions:

1. Fill a clean bowl with warm to hot water
2. Add 6-12 drops of the essence
3. Take a thin cloth at least 6 in by 6 in or whatever size covers your body zone
4. Place the cloth in the hot water. Let it sit for at least 10 seconds, then grab tongs to pull out of the hot water. Ring leaving moisture but not enough that it will drip
5. Apply to body zones of pain or discomfort that came up in the body check exercise. Use it to compress or pain vacuum specific zones i.e. chakra zones
6. Cover with a towel

7. Optional- cover with a heat pack for long term compression

8. Go lay down horizontal for at least 45 minutes.

9. When you are complete perform the body check & see what has shifted

Key 3- Spine Flower Power

Spine specific applications are an excellent method to use with cotton balls or direct from the bottle. Using the cotton ball method will usually yield an easier integration of the essences into the PEMS. Direct from the bottle applications tend to be used for those who have a tougher constitution and need more saturation to create longer lasting changes. This is an excellent method for transforming your personal essence soul KEY i.e. your big life lesson that you need to learn over and over again at deeper more profound levels. It is most often what you are constantly striving to be better at.

This method is like a battery jump start for the entire PEMS system and like any battery jump it can go easily or it can be overpowering. If you are at all nervous about doing this method after reading the above statement, then you are not currently ready for this method. Go back to keys one and two to see which one you are most attracted to. Then start there and work your way back to this application. In time, your PEMS system will have raised in vibration to another plane of consciousness so that your sustainable beauty can shine.

Warning: Most often is the case with this mountain moving application, a type of healing ascension will occur in the PEMS. Please give yourself time to settle into your new PEMS being and integrate all the changes by taking a break from the essences if you need to. Other times, violet can be used to mop up all the changes that have shaken themselves loose for a shadow pack Mirror review. This will allow you to integrate deeply and purge all that is not serving to the PEMS.

Spine Application Directions:

- *Perform a body check and create a body inventory to help you choose which essence will support your system the most during this timeframe Create a treatment cup with warm water and add the chosen one drop of essence.* Then dip in a cotton ball and gently squeeze out any excessive water by squeezing your fingers together at the top of the cotton ball. *Apply to the spine* by placing the cotton ball at the top of spine and squeeze out the warmly enhanced water out of the middle and front of the cotton ball. *Allow the liquid to trail down the spine* and either soak into your clothes or underwear line for long term compression or when unclothed allow the essence to soak into the body by air drying. The essence will not stain clothes as long as it is diluted with water and applied with the cotton ball method.

Direct Drop Spine Application:

This particular method is very strong! It is pure essence rolling down the most sensory and motor aspects of your being. It will create large shifts in your system and some extreme cases deep purging until a new vital plane is accomplished.

- *Perform a body check. Apply to the spine* by dropping 1-3 drops of the chosen essence top of spine (where your neck creases). *Allow the liquid to trail slowly down the spine. Note this method takes longer to apply as the pure essence moves its ways at a snail pace down the spine until it reaches the hips. Perform a body check and see what shifted or is calling for more attention.*

Chapter 10 Week 5- Water Power

Water, Hydrotherapy, and Bath uses are excellent resources for any ascending system. They work well in combination with a multitude of other applications and lend to the synergistic effect of self-awareness. Water and vibrational or energy medicines work synergistically with water to drive the essence into the spaces surrounding each cell. By working in this zero point, the vibrational healing properties can directly communicate with the PEMS system as a whole.

We know that water therapy or hydrotherapy has a deeply therapeutic effect on the PEMS systems. When water is combined with other therapies or modalities, a synergistic effect is created. This means that if you were to use each of the therapies or modalities alone, you would get an expected outcome of x or what we will assign as #2. If you added all your modalities together, say you were using these three: Essences, Hydrotherapy & Salts. You would expect the answer to be 6. However when these work together synergistically, we can expect to see a higher outcome than 6. This is the epitome of the sum of the parts is less than the whole.

Hydrotherapy and the essences increase the PEMS ability to absorb the vibrational qualities into all of the PEMS. This allows the system to do a lot of work in a short amount of time. We are utilizing the infinite potential of water and blending it with set intention, sacred geometry, plant spirit medicine and color therapy to communicate with these highly intelligent systems.

Each key below builds upon the many uses of water power towards the goal of self-healing. Use one or all the keys in this chapter to support your PEMS in its transformation.

Key 1- Drinking Water Power

The easiest way to start changing your personal waters is to work with essences and quantum infusions with a higher vibration than you. By drinking water infused with intelligence and intent, you get to start reprogramming your internal waters with self-reflection and active re-patterning. By infusing your daily drinking water with a new color or essence, you will actively raise your vibration. Increasing your bio-frequency and allowing you and your internal physician to more easily activate your water powers of self-healing.

Choose one color or essence to work with each day and use the quantum infusion using the color boards at the back of the book. Here is a refresher from last week.

NOTE- if you do not have the CannaEssences to work with. You can use the Quantum infusion technique as a replacement for the essences see below. Then use in the preparations below.

1. ***Quantum Infused Intelligent Water– Use within 12 Hours***

    Use your core four color boards at the back of the book to make activated to intelligent water using your CannaEssence color board. Is all you will need is a small glass of water. You can then use this in replacement of drops of essence below. A quantum infusion is less powerful than the actual essence. However it will be of some use as you activate your intention, imagination, and imagery towards your final goals of self-healing and elevating your environment.

Perform a personal body check to get a sense of the PEMS and its needs today at this moment. With the core four master flower color boards in hands with eyes closed or soft gaze, ask what one color will support you most and then open your eyes and gaze at your color boards. Does one color or picture stand out from the rest? Perhaps it looks brighter than the others, or your eye is just drawn back towards that one image. Place your small glass of water on top of the image you choose for at least 20 minutes to allow your intelligent water to infuse. Use within twelve hours. For every drop of essence that the recipe calls for you will use one teaspoon of the prepared and activated waters.

Key 2- Bath Power

The power of the bath has gone back to the beginning of human recorded history. Famous baths from the Romans and Greeks have worked their way into our imagination with tales of a luxury community. When self-healing the power of the bath is not to be ignored. The healing waters work directly with your PEMS to increase your vibration. A variety of techniques can be used to make the bath perfect for your system. The bath can be increased in potency and vibration by adding other ingredients to the healing waters.

Choose one or a combination of healing baths below. The combinations are endless, and the vibrational potential is boundless.

1. **Quantum Infused Bath –**

Use your core four color boards at the back of the book to make an activated or intelligent water using your CannaEssence color board. Is all you will need is a small glass of water to add to your bath after the quantum infusion.

Perform a personal body check to get a sense of the PEMS and its needs today at this moment. With the core four master flower color boards in hands with eyes closed or soft gaze, ask what one color will support you most and then open your eyes and gaze at your color boards. Does one color or picture stand out from the rest? Perhaps it looks brighter than the others, or your eye is just drawn back towards that one image. Pick up the bottle and take with you into the bathroom. Draw yourself a bath and place your small glass of water on top of the image for at least 20 minutes. At this point, you can add Salts, Essential oil or Herbal infusions to increase the synergistic effects of the parts to create something superbly supportive. *Add your quantum infusion after the twenty minutes to your drawn bath. Sink into the tub letting your physical, emotional, mental and spiritual bodies be infused with the pristine vibrational imprint & color of your choosing. Breathe it into your lungs filling them with the color of choice. Feeding, nourishing and caretaking for the blood that is being oxygenated and then shunted to various parts of the body. Creating a chain reaction of cell color, until the entire body is light with color. Transforming what was letting what is now shining with renewed grace, beauty and clarity. Perform a body check and notice any changes in sensations or discomfort. Close. Cleanup.*

2. *CannaEssence in the Bath Directions- Optional Bottles use:*

CannaEssence in the bath is a lovely support to PEMS vacuuming. By using the essences mindfully in the bath you its potential for transformation as you co-create mindfulness. If you combine the CannaEssences along with other bath applications you can increase the potency of the self-love session. Many clients have raved about the "beauty" aspects to using the essences in the bath. I frequently hear remarks like, "people say I look more radiant", "I'm glowing", "I look younger", "I just look different, more me." This is the benefit of PEMS awareness and reconnection to the whole system.

Perform a personal body check to get a sense of the PEMS and its needs today in this moment. Eyes closed or soft gaze, ask what one essence will support you most and then open your eyes and gaze at your essences. Does one color or picture stand out from the rest? Perhaps it looks brighter than the others or your eye is just drawn back towards that one bottle. Pick up the bottle and take with you into the bathroom. Draw yourself a bath and use 3-12 drops of an essence per bathtub of water. Less drops for those who are sensitive to the essences and 12 drops for those who sense less from the essences. At this point you can add Salts, Essential oil or Herbal infusions to increase the synergistic effects of the parts to create something superbly supportive. *Sink into the tub letting your physical, emotional, mental and spiritual bodies be infused with the pristine vibrational imprint & color of your choosing. Breathe it into your lungs filling them with the color of choice. Feeding, nourishing and caretaking for the blood that is being oxygenated and then shunted to various parts of the body. Creating a chain reaction of cell color, until the entire body is a light with color. Transforming what was letting what is now shining with renewed grace, beauty and clarity. Perform a body check and notice any changes in sensations or discomfort. Close. Cleanup.*

3. *Salts in the Bath Directions:*

Salt has a natural ability to drive the vibrational qualities right to the core of a cell through cellular diffusion. By utilizing the nature of salt, water and the human condition we are able to deeply transform the PEMS from the inside of each cell. Salts with an origin in the sea have a higher tendency to more resonate vibrations that create longer lasting changes then iodized or table salt. By using a ¼ cup of Dead Sea salt, sea salt, pink Himalayan sea salt, black volcano sea salt or other varieties you too can increase yourself care sessions. Epsom salt is a nice neutral middle range resonance quality. I think of the salt vibrational qualities in order of least resonant (powerfully transformative) to most resonant: Table salt/iodized, Epsom, black volcano sea salt, Dead Sea, Pink Himalayan, Celtic sea salt and the highest resonancy of Sustainable gathered sea salt. There are many more versions of sea salt out there; I encourage you to explore what the sea world has to offer your system so you can find a perfect resonance match for your PEMS.

> *Add ¼ cup of Epsom, Dead Sea or other sea salts to purify & increase the potency of the essence chosen as you are drawing your bath. Swirl around with your arm or foot before sinking in and soaking on top of the non-dissolved salts. After the bath, let your body & hair air dry, soaking in all the minerals. Once your body is fully dry you can take a rinse off and wash your hair with a small amount of leave-in moisturizing conditioner.*

*Warning: Non-dissolved sea salts can be extremely irritating to the skin. Watch for sitting directly on the non-dissolved salts. If you experience burning or caustic sensations get up and dissolve the salt into the water more thoroughly before sitting back down. Suggest a heavy water rinse before sitting back down to avoid lasting irritation.

4. *Mineral Kingdom - Stones & Gems in the Bath Directions:*

It is well known in the metaphysical world, that minerals, gems and stones have healing qualities that when combined with water and salt to resonate vibratory qualities into the surrounding area. As we learn more about physics and our Universe, minerals are taking on an archetypical quality that can be harnessed to serve humanities ascension process in the form of gem essences. By using stones, gems and minerals in the bath you are creating a gem essence. By adding this powerful ally to your CannaEssence bath you can potentize the synergistic effects of flowers, gems, water and salt.

> *Place the stone over the drain stopper and let the bath pour its fresh water over the stone, infusing it with its healing qualities.* If you want to add: salts, essence, essential oils, teas

etc do so when the tub is ¼ way full. *Add stones, gems or minerals to increase the potency and provide a catalyst to the flower & color essence.*

5. *Herbal Teas, Tisanes & Infusions in the Bath Directions:*

Herbal teas in the bath are such a wonderful addition to the conscious ascending human. By using the healing qualities of the herb in combination with CannaEssence, Sea salts, stones & gems you can create a perfectly tuned resonance resource for your own PEMS system. An herbal bath can be stronger or subtle to suit your personal needs. If you would like it to be stronger you will need to use more herbs and at least a 2 quart cooking pot. Subtle can be as little as a few drops, tablespoons or cup. It will all depend on what you have on hand as well as your personal tastes and PEMS needs. If you have sturdy tea bags your tea can be directly infused into the bath.

Flowers and leaves have a tendency to be more aromatic then their underground friends the roots as well as their tougher aerial protectors the barks and the tough babies the seeds for the next generation. Flowers & leaves are aromatic and contain a portion of volatile or essential oils. This means that if you heat them the vapors will dissipate out as the herb infuses over its 5-7 timeframe or when exposed to boiling water. I suggest that you cover your herbs so that no aromatic properties are released before you want them to be i.e. in your bath and your nostrils filling the room with the subtle aroma of your chosen herbal ally.

Roots, seeds, barks tend to be tougher than their sensitive aerial or above ground friends flowers, leaves and stems. This means that they can be exposed to higher temperatures of heat before releasing their volatile or essential oils. I still like to cover my herbal bath infusions and decoctions because it almost guarantees that I will be the recipient of the herbal aromatics and not my entire environment. Now go and co-create with your PEMS system for self care goodness.

> *Subtle Infusion for flowers and leaves: Take 1 teabag of any herb of your choice or 1-2 tablespoons of loose herb and pour 1 cup of boiling water over the herb. Cover and let steep at least 5-7 minutes. Strain to remove herb if necessary. Once the brew is complete, add herbal infusion to bath as it is drawing into the CannaEssence bath. Sink in and enjoy your resonance tailored bath.* If you are enjoying the tea and

completed your cup before the bath drew ☺ you can pour boiling water over the previously used herbs with another cup of boiling water, let it steep and take ½ cup and pour strained tea into the tub

Subtle Decoction for roots, seeds and barks: Use a small saucepan with 2.5 cups of water with loose roots, seeds or barks. Usually, you will need at least two heaping tablespoons roughly a small handful of cut and sifted herb. Put all the ingredients in the saucepan with cool water on medium heat gently simmering for at least 45 minutes. You will lose roughly half of the original liquid with an expected volume of 1 cup. After 45 minutes, strain into a clean glass, ceramic holding vessel or directly into the CannaEssence bath. You can pour new water over the herb and let it simmer as you soak in the bath. Once done you can enjoy internally the goodness of your creation is a subtle manner. Adding honey to taste, coconut milk, etc. can be a pleasant addition to the self-care process. Sink in and enjoy your personally tailored bath.

Strong Infusion for flowers and leaves: Use at least a 2-quart saucepan with boiling water and a lid. Once boiling, add no less than 1 cup of flowers, leaves & stems of the herb of your choice and put the lid on. Immediately, move the covered pot to cool burner and set a timer to let sit for 45 minutes to overnight. The longer you let the brew sit and infuse the stronger it will become in the 12 hour use period. Refrigerate overnight in warm weather once cool to the touch.

Strong Decoction for roots, seeds, and barks: Use a 2-quart saucepan with cool water and a lid with at least ¼ cup - ½ cup loose roots, seeds or barks. Usually, you will need at least ¼ cup for a strong 2-quart decoction. Put all the ingredients in the saucepan with cool water on medium heat gently simmering for at least 45 minutes. You will lose roughly half of the original liquid with an expected volume of 1 cup. After 45 minutes, strain into a clean glass, ceramic holding vessel or directly into the CannaEssence bath. You can pour new water over the herb and let it simmer as you soak in the bath.

6. *Essential & Volatile Oils in the Bath Directions:*

By utilizing the pleasant aspects of aromatherapy and its proven therapeutic benefits you can synergize your CannaEssence bath to the highest resonancy by combining multiple bath resources. CannaEssence + water + essential oil + salts + herbal infusion = powerhouse of transformation and PEMS integration. Essential oils must never be dropped directly into a bath without diluting them in a carrier oil. It can be extremely painful and damaging to the delicate mucosal and nerve endings of the anus and genitals.

Carrier oils can be any cooking oil like extra virgin olive oil, sesame, grape seed, hemp, etc. Cosmetic grade oils like macadamia, hazelnut, almond, avocado, evening primrose, etc. There are so many to choose from, however cooking oil is usually the easiest thing to find in anyones cabinet. Otherwise, most health food stores and specialty online suppliers will carry the other oils mentioned.

Add up to 16 drops of a high-quality essential oil to 2 tablespoons of carrier oil in a cup or shot glass. Add this mix to the bath as it is drawing about ¼ to ½ way full.

Key 3- Energy Partner & Water Power

By utilizing the support of an energy partner, you increase your ability to create deep self-healing. All healing happens in a relationship and by using the support of another person you are allowing your system to be authentic and free. I love to use these exercises to increase my healing potential or when I have been doing a lot of self-work.

The below exercises can be used when you are experiencing upset in the system or need a deep integration.

1. *Overhead Hydrotherapy Sitting in a Bath– Co-Creative Hydrotherapy Directions:*

Overhead hydrotherapy is a way of recreating a gentle waterfall from nature in your bathtub with the help of an energy partner. The energy partner will be in control of the speed and flow of the waterfall. You can increase the potency of the hydrotherapy by combining multiple bath resources CannaEssence + Herbal Infusion = potent gentle waters. This is an excellent way to utilize the power of 2 people working towards the same intentional goal. By using the heart space to facilitate change with intention massive changes in the PEMS can occur. Get together and create a shared intention to support and serve the transformation of PEMS through hydrotherapy. This type of application can be very cleansing, supportive and tends to move energy around your PEMS in a vortex of release. This is one of my favorite ways of receiving essences with an energy partner. Very useful for those who are recovering or needing a bit of gentle support for the entire PEMS system.

A few words of wisdom to the energy partner: Please utilize this as an opportunity to serve the person receiving. It is a great opportunity to co-create with your energy partner as you witness the metamorphosis that water can bring to the entire PEMS system. Stay present with them, watch for small cues that show discomfort or a desire to speak up but needing some support. You will be holding a great space or bubble of intention for serving your energy partner. Your job is to facilitate the container or space to help serve their needs through overhead hydrotherapy.

You will need a comfortable pouring vessel for the energy partner. When choosing a vessel it should be: easy to handle, hold a decent amount of fluid, weighted for the person using it i.e. not too heavy, easy to grip. Think, can I lift this 100x? If the answer is no you should probably keep searching. I suggest a quart mason jar with 2 or 3 rubber bands wrapped around the outside to provide some gripping. I have also used jar opener rubber tools to perform the overhead hydrotherapy more easily. A bulbous vase for larger bouquets works nicely as well. It is imperative to fill the bath to fit the vessel, for example, if you choose a larger vase you will need to fill the bath much fuller than ½ bath more like ¾ to full.

*Warning of caution: Be very careful if you use essential oils or mineral salts as these can get into the eyes and cause challenges. I tend to just use: CannaEssence + Herbal infusion with great results.

Directions for the Person Receiving the Overhead Hydrotherapy: Perform a body check in view of your essence set. Choose which essence or essences will serve you most today. Read about the essence with your energy partner. Choose some intentions you would like your energy partner to hold for you. What support do you feel you need right now? *Discuss with your energy partner. Draw the bath at least ½ way full with your preferred water temperature. You can choose to wear a bathing suit or be present in the nude according to your comfort level with your energy partner and personal preference. Get relaxed in a bath, with your spine accessible to your energy partner. Have your energy partner pour vase after vase of water over your head and down your spine. Keeping your shared intention + essence chosen + any other intentions you wish to have support as the water cascades over your PEMS. Let them know if you would the water to be slower, faster or whatever serves your PEMS sensations. Your energy partner may pour 10x or 100xs it is all up to what your system needs. Note: If you are consistently drawn towards the 100x mark then I suggest doing a compression application after your overhead hydrotherapy with the same color for long-lasting changes with your friend water + CannaEssence.*

Directions for the energy partner: Help run the person receiving a body check. Have them ask their system which one essence or color will serve them most today? Have them open their eyes and choose the essence that best serves their PEMS today. Read about the essence description. Ask what they would like you to hold as your shared intention. Reiterate and speak back to them how you understand their intention to clarify you are both on the same page about their intentions and needs. Help draw a bath to at least ½ - ¾ full according to the pouring vessel. Invite your receiving energy partner to get comfortable in the bath. Inquire as to how they would you like you to start the pouring process? Dip your vessel into the bathtub and fill it up then take it and reverently pour it gently over the crown of your partners head and down their spine. If the vessel is unable to fill all the way you should drawn more water into the bath until it is easier to fill and pour. *Continue to intently watch for signs or cues for you to change or modify your pour to serve the needs of the person in front of you. Continue to pour over the system with your shared intention in mind.* If this falters, check in with your energy partner. See if there is anything they would like you do differently to better serve their intentions? *After 10-100x pours your partner will most likely sense completion if the shared intention.* Once they sense this completion or closing, you can thank them for letting you witness their transformation and politely excuse yourself from the bathroom, trying the lights down, and encouraging them to soak in the tub until done. You can then go and prepare a small meal or beverage to discuss or you can simply close and go back to your own home, safely locking them in their abode.

2. *Constitutional Hydrotherapy or Full Body Hydrotherapy Directions:*

Constitutional hydrotherapy is my absolute favorite method to help in any crisis state during or after an ascension period. This is especially useful when the PEMS system is heightened in its sensitivity and there is a sense of rawness to the world around you. Nerves may be feeling exposed and the system is wanting to retreat and hide from the world. It can be used for any type of whole body integration that is requiring a full body rewiring. A must have after any ascension period for a highly sensitive person (HSP). I consider this a type of rescue or acute support that resets the entire PEMS system. Extremely useful at resetting any frazzled nervous system, PEMS overload, trauma resolution and triggers.

*When used for integration it is best to not include essences as the system is already in flux state.

*If you are using this to increase the potency of an essence or color you would add 12 drops of the chosen essence to the bath.

> *Take a warm to hot shower for at least 5-7 minutes or a bath with soaking time of at least 7-10 minutes.* You can have your energy partner come in and pour vases of water over the top of your head with it washing down your spine. *After bath, without drying off, have someone take a sheet wrapping you up like a burrito. Then your energy partner will cover you with a blanket and help you get to horizontal position (lying down). Rest for 45-90 minutes depending on your personal needs. Once you are dry your full body hydrotherapy session is complete. You may rest as long as your PEMS needs. Close. Unwrap your system & dress or go to bed and integrate all those momentous shifts.*

Chapter 11 **Week 6- Wild Power**

Key 1- Activate Your Intuition & Create a Self Healing Plan

Energetic resonancy is a technique used to find harmony between two or more separate frequencies. I like to use a dousing tool or my finger to find the energetic resonancy for my PEMS. This form will allow you to choose a tool to work with that will match and elevate your resonancy to whole other level. Energetic resonancy requires that you trust your internal physician who is speaking through your finger or dousing rod. The goal is to find the best self-healing Cannabis energy medicine plan that meets your needs at this particular moment. The form breaks down color, CannaEssence, treatment types, duration of treatment. With this tool, you could easily create a protocol to activate your wild powers of intuition, vibration, and frequency.

When you are looking for energetic resonancy with your finger, you are sensing with your PEMS and present powers the harmonic frequency that makes your finger vibrate and hum almost as if filled with life and vitality. You will need to go slow and sense with all of your PEMS senses. Noticing small changes and vibrations that call your attention. This is not a trick it is your body connecting through the holographic quantum field and resonating with the tools that will elevate your consciousness.

Energetic Resonancy & Dousing Form

These forms you can use with your dowsing tool or your body as a dousing rod or energetic resonancy gauge. You can close your eyes or use a soft gaze after doing your body check to get you heart centered and prepared to listen to your body cues for resonancy. This resonancy is what will guide partner energy sessions or self-care sessions. This is the easiest form to use as it is never wrong even if you were way off on what you thought you needed before the session then during the session something else came up, and you got different answers for your after session review.

Steps to work with the energetic resonancy and dousing form:

1. Body check

2. Write name & date

3. Choose dowsing or energetic resonancy

4. Picture the person who you are visualizing the dosage for- you or another person

5. Ask their higher source what essence would be best serving to them at this moment?

6. Then run your finger or dousing tool over the CannaEssence & Color Choices form

    a. Mark any that get a yes answers, have a heavy or dragging sensation, holding back from going forward and more. Trust your intuition here and just write down what comes first. You can always do a before and after compare session and see how resonant you were

        i. with your client or self when you are complete

7. Now that you know which essences & colors you need, you will have to figure out the dosing duration in days or months for each essence or color you choose

    a. *To do this, you will need to place your finger on the block you choose & visualize the color or essence and ask your body or the resonancy between you and another's source how long they will need to take this particular essence. Then run your finger over the duration section marking in the essence or color box the duration. Continue to do this for all of your essences or colors*

8. You will follow the above steps for each color and essence with focus on how to best apply the essence or color for your systems or your resonancy partners system

    a. *This is an exercise that can take a bit of practice to feel comfortable doing it as it requires trust in your intuition and the cues that you are getting. These can be extremely subtle, so much so that many folks will dismiss them. That is why the before and after is so cool. As you get to know what's you and what's your resonancy with an essence or color things will become easy and clarified. Just give yourself time, a break and have fun with the exploration!*

CannaEssence™ ENERGETIC RESONANCY & DOUSING FORM

Clients Name:
Practitioner:
Date:

Before   or   After   session   – circle please

Essences	SB	GC	GG	HB	EB	JB	BB	DP	PK	OG	MK	BJ
Colors	Red	Ora	Yell	Lime	Green	Em	Turq	Blu	Indi	Purp	Vio	Mage
DOSING **Duration**	1	2	3	4	5	6	7	8	9	10	11	12
Days to be *used*	13	14	15	16	17	18	19	20	21	22	23	24
	25	26	27	28	29	30	31	MORE: 6 weeks 8 weeks 3month				
Frequency *X per day*	1	2	3	4	5	6	7	8	9	10	11	12
Application **Type**	Drops Intern	Auric Infuse	Bath	Lotion cream	Spong FB	Cotton Ball	Lotion	Oil	Aloe Vera	Spray Mist	Compress	Reflex
How to **Apply**	Full Body	Focus Area	Direct	Pain Zone	Spine	Full Body	Internal Drops					

Key 2- Make Your Own Flower Power

Make Your Own Flower Essence

Supplies needed: bowl, scissors, tweezers, strainers, funnels, water, brandy, brown/blue or green dropper bottles for mother, stock, and dosage bottles

The Sun Method is the most Common:

Directions: *Use clear glass and tweezers if you'd like or a leaf from the plant itself. Sit with the plant and ask permission for medicine. Pluck flowers with tweezers or hands covered in a leaf to protect and keep separate your vibration from that of the remedy you are trying to make. You can also place flowers still attached to plant into the bowl of water. I tend to cover the surface of the water with the most precious & vital flowers leaving the wilting or day old flowers to turn to seeds on the stalk.*

Let the flowers sit in direct sunlight for a minimum ½ hour up to 24 hours. Usually, 4 hours is a good average time for powerful essences. I look for the bubbles in the water & the wilting of the flowers. Early morning tends to be the best for making flower essences. Being out in the early am keeps the bugs out of your water as they are not usually flying around till 11am-12pm. Watch out. Bees are attracted to the flowers.

Once the flowers life force is transferred into the living activated water, you will want to capture the essence into the form of a mother. See chapter two for definitions of terms.

Strain the flowers from the water using the strainer, into a clean dropper bottle fill half way full with essence and the other half with brandy. This will be your Mother essence. All your stock bottles will be created using one dropper full roughly thirty drops of essence per ½ oz bottle, then fill it the rest of the way full with brandy. The stock bottle then dispenses 1-3 drops of essence into a dosage bottle to be taken over the course of one week or one lunar cycle as seen in week four.

Key 3- Elevate Your Environment

The garden is a great place to watch Nature at work in all her glory. Any seasoned gardener will tell you that plants have an all out war during the growing season. Some plants are dominant and fast growing, taking nutrients from the other slower, shallower root systems. This leaves an abundance of dominant plants while the others are slowly strangled and killed. This war is why we" pull weeds" to "save" other plants, so that they can grow and produce vegetables or fruit. As a biodynamic urban gardener, I tend to have a wild looking garden; that is a place where the war can easily be seen to be sustainable and nourishing to the cohabiting plants. I always choose to plant my garden with companion plants. This way my garden, when it goes wild as it inevitably will, will create its own soil system that serves the entire ecosystem. By using flower essences to support my garden, I can change the way a plant behaves to its neighbors and pests. The CannaEssences serve to tame them with love and nourishment, so that the war turns to a peace treaty of co-creation and cohabitation.

When I have pests going after a certain plant i.e. tomatoes I will go and observe the area during the three main parts of the day i.e. morning, afternoon and the evening right before sundown. Then I will ask the plants which essences will serve them, to balance the plants PEMS system, so that they can better fend off pest and predators. The plant spirit then indicates through subtle communication methods its needs and desires. Those who listen to this unique voice will get clear indications on what are the next steps to creating vital health. This plant spirit voice can come to each person in a slightly different manner.

In my experience, the way people first start to sense plant spirits energies is through their most dominant learning style. However for many, especially during their first experiences, there will be an inner knowing of what the plant is trying to tell you, however being new and untrusting you may think you heard nothing at all. It's a trick; your senses will tell you exactly what to do. There is no needs to think about it- just trust this intuition and keep practicing active listening and observation. For others it will take much practice to TRUST what you are sensing with your PEMS. The best way to start is to sit for 10 minutes in front of one plant and notice all the little details of this plant that has caught your attention. If you are called to make a quick sketch, it may serve to deepen the interaction between your PEMS and the plant spirits PEMS.

Birds and wildlife love the essences. Any range or brand you are attracted to will bring you the support in your garden that you need. This is the magic of the law of attraction and color psychology. You will always choose what you need the most in the moment therefore giving your system the perfect support in its greatest need. By adding essences to bird and animal water, the animal kingdom is supported and balanced to your gardens perfect harmony. This creates a great resonance for you, the animals and the plants. In gardens where this co-creation has been part of the very fabric of its growth for 3+ years; they have a special energy and quantum signature. I noticed more bees, less pests and more cohabitation between all species. It was almost as if the whole ecosystem was working towards the optimal goal of conscious, sustainable and beautiful gardening just like I was. In my clients yards, where they said nothing would grow, they have thriving gardens full of abundant wildlife and co diversity.

NOTE- if you do not have the CannaEssences to work with. You can use the Quantum infusion technique as a replacement for environmental work.

1. *Quantum Infused Intelligent Water– Use within 12 Hours*

    Use your core four color boards at the back of the book to make an activated to intelligent water using your CannaEssence color board. Is all you will need is a small glass of water. You can then use this in replacement of drops of essence below. A quantum infusion is less powerful than the actual essence, however it will be of some use as you activate your intention, imagination and imagery towards your final goals of self-healing and elevating your environment.

Perform a personal body check to get a sense of the PEMS and its needs today in this moment. With the core four master flower color boards in hands with eyes closed or soft gaze, ask what one color will support you most and then open your eyes and gaze at your color boards. Does one color or picture stand out from the rest? Perhaps it looks brighter than the others or your eye is just drawn back towards that one image. Place your small glass of water on top of the image for at least 20 minutes to allow your intelligent water to infuse. Use within twelve hours. For every drop of essence that the recipe calls for you will use 1 teaspoon of the prepared and activated waters.

1. *Using Essences in the Watering Can*

   This is one of the most diverse ways to use the essences with your garden. The essences are very powerful to the plant kingdom. The water has a special communication system with plants that needs very little essence to create large changes in the plants PEMS systems. This is part of the quantum bio-resonance communication complex. Add this water to any plant that needs a little bit of special attention.

   Focused Plant- Acute Care: Take a moment to look really at the plant that wants some special attention. Get up close. Notice any injuries, weeping spots, bugs, or any other details that stick out at you. Once you have a good sense of what is going on in the plants PEMS system; look at your CannaEssence set and choose the color or flower that you are most attracted. *Add 1-3 drops of essence to any size water can or mister or sprayer. I suggest a mix of the two for an acute case or a plant that wants special attention. Mist the leaves 3x a day for three days.* Water the plant with a little bit of Essence enhanced water. *If the plant likes a big drink; water as you normally would. If you water 1-3x a week, just make a new essence enhanced watering can for each watering day. If you have a plant that only likes a tiny drink. You can freeze up essence enhanced ice cubes in any standard ice tray. Giving the plant 1 to 3 ice cubes each day for three days.* This will depend on the size of your plant's water demands. Please stop watering if mold or fuzz appears. Allow the plant to dry out and then try another essence. This is a type of plant acute care. Sometimes they need a little surgery to skim off the top non-serving layer of dirt and have a new layer or healthy dirt infusion. ☺ Listen to your plant spirit friends and they will show you the way to vital plants.

2. *Watering According to the Color Days of the Week:*
   Purple- Monday is, Violet- Monday pm, Red- Tuesday, Yellow- Wednesday, Orange- Thursday, Green- Friday, Indigo- Saturday, Magenta- Sunday

3. *Using Essences in Hydroponics*

I have been receiving many case reports from Colorado grow operations on the use of the CannaEssences with their crops. Some report decreased pest and more vital plants. Once we gather more information and case reports on this use, I will report it in my second edition.

Sit with your plants or current group of grows. Cannabis grows, or species specific grows- you will want to tailor your daily mix to the needs of your plants. This will require sitting with the plants for a while as you listen to their PEMS collective needs. During this time you may notice that a specific plant may need some acute or immediate attention and it may not be the same as the rest of the group. See above Focused Plant- Acute Care. *Once you know the essence that the group would like to use, you can add 1-3 drops to your master tank. Allow your plants to flush as normal. Repeat the next time you fill your master tank.*

4. *Using Essences in Animal Water*

Animals, like the plants, are very sensitive to energetic vibrations. This means that a little goes a long way to making PEMS transformations. By paying attention and doing some Nature watching you will be able to figure out which essence will serve your animal kingdom friends the best in your ecosystem.

Add one drop of the chosen essence to the animal watering dish or bowl. I like to start in my garden with abundance and then move through the colors according to the needs of the animals.

5. *Using Essences as a Pest Deterrent*

You can use the essences as a natural barrier to pests on top of infusing the plants PEMS with fortitude and abundance. I like to use Violet – Cleansing as a barrier or pest deterrent. I have infused salt, water, placed drops on rocks, used the four directions and added to my roof and trees. This use of diluted and direct drops created a type of network that wove webbing around my gardens ecosystem; a special little paradise in the city. By combining both the exterior protection and internal watering of the plants using the above method we can see huge changes in the garden ecosystem.

Direct Drop Pest Deterrent Method: Take one drop and put it in the four directions of your house; on the edge of your property line. This forms a square around your house. *Then get on top your roof and place one drop at the middle or topmost section of your roof. If you do not have a roof; place one drop directly in the middle of the garden.* Do not endanger yourself i.e. get on the chimney. This has created a 3D pyramid around your garden. You just performed a type of quantum cleansing using Sacred Geometry + Essences + Colors = VibroChromoTherapy.

Diluted Drops & Watering Can Barrier Method: Take a large watering can with a thin neck and drop three drops into the water. Then go to the edge of your property and start walking as you trail a thin fountain of barrier water around your home. You may need to fill 3+ cans to complete this method for a standard suburban home. Just go back to where you left off and connect the water lines as you continue to work your way around your property to where you began. Once you are complete with this process, it should last at least one lunar cycle sometimes up to 3+ months for well-maintained gardens with daily enhanced water through the growing season.

Chapter 12 Resources

All your downloadable content can be picked up in one easy package by emailing a picture of your purchase receipt to:

Info@CannaEssence.org

Essence Resources- Suppliers

- ✓ Bach – English Essences http://www.fesflowers.com/healing_herbs.htm

- ✓ CannaEssences http://www.CannaEssence.org or Colorado local Retailers

- ✓ Alaskan Essences http://www.alaskanessences.com

- ✓ Perelandra – garden & rose essences http://www.perelandra-ltd.com/

- ✓ FES- flower essence society flower sets – http://wwwifesflowers.com

- ✓ Dessert Essences – Mimi Kamp - https://essenceofthedesert.wordpress.com/bio/

Kirlian Photography Resources

Full Spectrum Presentations http://www.fullspectrum.org.uk/index.php/about-us/

Chapter 13 FAQ's
Most Commonly Asked Questions & Answers Q & A

What are Flower Essences?

Flower essences (FE) have a famed reputation as some of the most effective, least intrusive, & safest remedies in our vast pharmacopeia. Flower essence is a type of energy medicine that is very similar to Homoeopathy. FEs contains no scent and can be used internally & externally. Most flower essences are described as the vibrational imprints or maps left from the spirit of the plant. Flower essences are known to impact greatly all facets of your being when used with intention & mindfulness including the *PEMS – Physical/body, emotional, mental and spirit.*

Do The Essences Contain THC or CBDs?

No, CannaEssences are the first flower essences of the cannabis plant that do not contain any THC or CBDs. *You will NOT test positive* for a drug test as these are the components that flag a positive drug analysis whether its urine, blood or hair.

Will I Test Positive on a Drug Test?

No, there are no THC or CBD components to trigger a positive result on a drug test.

How Do Vibrational Remedies Work?

Vibrational remedies work by balancing the human energy system by providing support and mindfulness to the self-reflection and assessment process. This webbing of support builds on the previous "work" that has been done to move dysfunction and disease out of the system. Vibrational remedies work deeply with the law of attraction and synchronicity.

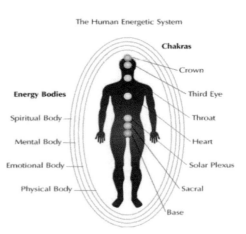

What is the PEMS System?

The human PEMS system consists of the Physical human body, the Emotional body, the Mental body and the Spiritual bodies shown in the picture as well as your understanding of these terms. The PEMS, when calibrated with the hearts intelligence and bioelectric field, will balance each one of these systems. This is a unique way of thinking of the PEMS systems for it leaves it all in your control of your association or attraction to what this term means to you. In the book, we are referring to these bodies or their representation in the human life expression. For example, when thoughts circulate in my mental body I sense them in my physical body as heaviness and inflation of energy in my head. Therefore, my thoughts are affecting both my mental and physical bodies. Physiologically, there is a complex nervous system in the heart called the "heart brain" that interconnects the heart & the brain with its two way superhighway.

How Does the Heart Field Affect the Geomagnetic Field?

Howard Martin from the Institute of Heart Math and a large team of researchers are working on collecting large amounts of data all over the world to prove or disprove their working hypothesis. We know that the Earths Geomagnetic fields affect the human electromagnetic or bioelectric field and that they have some interrelationship. However, that relationship is not yet fully understood. Therefore the Heart Math team has hypothesized that the human electromagnetic field may influence the Earth geomagnetic field in a positive or negative way. If this is true, that would mean that all the metaphysical view of my thoughts and emotions create patterns in my field that affect everything around me, and I'm affected by everything around me. As the research and data collection continue they hope to prove this inter-correlation so, that humans can start to come back to home and focus on themselves. If people raise their heart intelligence which in turn will modify and re-pattern their human electromagnetic field which in turn will re-pattern the Earth' geomagnetic field.

Why is it Important to Actively Work with Our Own Hearts Intelligence?

In this example from Heart Math, it displays each person's heart field. This heart field can accurately be measured from a few feet away from a person. Some folks call this their "energy bubble, aura field, heart torus, personal boundary, etc." this field interacts with everything you come interact with whether or not you are conscious of the interaction. This means that if your heart's intelligence can affect other people who are within a few feet of you whether or not you want to. This means that you must own your energy field and take responsibility for its effect on others.

Physics, Time Travel & the New Human Consciousness – The Connected Universe- The Matrix

An evolutionary imperative is occurring on our planet right now. It requires the way we perceive our consciousness both in our Science and our personal spiritual evolution, which may lead to a literal ascension of humankind into the Cosmos through space travel. Nassim Harramein is a revolutionary physicist who has given humanity an opportunity to study our world in a way we never thought possible, except in Star Trek of course. We now see, with our Science, that all things are interconnected by the spaces between points. This means that if we can tap into these spaces between the points, we can go to any other space between points in any dimension or time. Now that the linear model of the fabric of the universe has been disproven, we are searching for a new way to perceive ourselves and our place in the Universe. This means to us normal folk that inside of each of us and everything outside of ourselves has truly limitless, infinitesimal possibilities.

How Do I Display My Set?

These essences are best displayed in a window seal with diffused sunlight or a display unit with a LED display under the bottle. DO NOT PUT THE BOTTLES IN DIRECT SUNLIGHT. The colors on the bottles may fade due to direct sunlight.

If you have any other questions, please contact Info@CannaEssence.org

Chapter 14 CannaEssence Forms

Color Attraction Form

Pick the Flower You are Most Attracted to

CLEANSING

Deeply Cleansing & Rejuvenative

Renew, Refresh, & Revitalize

Leaves You Feeling: Uplifted, Alive, Radiant Connected to Source.

Use: When the physical, emotional, mental or spiritual bodies need a makeover or reset.

DESTINY'S CALLING

Trust spirit & your chosen path

The Pressures of Life Melt Away

Leaves You Feeling: Confident, Supported, Nourished, Focused, Relaxed, Loved.

Use: When your questioning your calling & life purpose, have racing thoughts, feel alone, confused, lost, disorganized or heart broken.

GROUNDING

Grounding & Energizing

Balance, Invigorate & Protect

Leaves You Feeling: Powerful, Energized, Balanced, Protected, Inner Peace.

Use: When you have low energy, exhaustion, fatigue, after traveling, illness or overdoing it. When needing to protect yourself from others emotions or actions.

ABUNDANCE

Manifest Prosperity

Renewed Joy, Safety, Love

Leaves You Feeling: Re-awakend Joy, Love, Compassion, Abundance, Prosperity.

Use: When a lack of abundance & prosperity are sensed. When feeling lonely, depressed, judgemental, impatient & frustrated with the world or themselves.

147

Personal Journal Form for the Core 4

Name: _____   Date: _____

6. <u>Are you currently experiencing any of the following?</u>

Pain/tenderness ❏ No ❏ Yes: **Stress** ❏ No ❏ Yes: **Allergies** ❏ No ❏ Yes   **Stiffness** ❏ No ❏ Yes:

Anxiety, Fear, Depression ❏ No ❏ Yes: **Numbness/tingling** ❏ No ❏ Yes: **Swelling** ❏ No ❏ Yes:

Mental suffering ❏ No ❏ Yes: **Emotional imbalance** ❏ No ❏ Yes: **New Consciousness** ❏ No ❏ Yes

7. **Which color or colors are you working with today?** *Circle one below*

Red_____   Green   Purple _____   Violet

8. Perform a body check before you use the essences. What do you notice in your PEMS? Please note any physical, emotional, mental or spiritual imbalances you are experiencing in the space & body below:

Before

Burning   *Tightness or discomfort*   *Ache*   *Sharp Pain*   *Numbness*   *Other*   *Aura/field Holes*

=====   *ooooooooooo*   *xxxx*   */////////*   *******   *zzzzz*   *Fill in with colors or drawings*

9. Choose an essence or application method & make sure to give those areas that came up in #3 a little more attention.

10. After your personal session, perform another body check and notice what has shifted and what still is asking for attention.

After

Burning	Tightness or discomfort	Ache	Sharp Pain	Numbness	Other	Aura/field Holes
=====	ooooooooooo	xxxx	/////////	*****	zzzzz	Fill in with colors or drawings

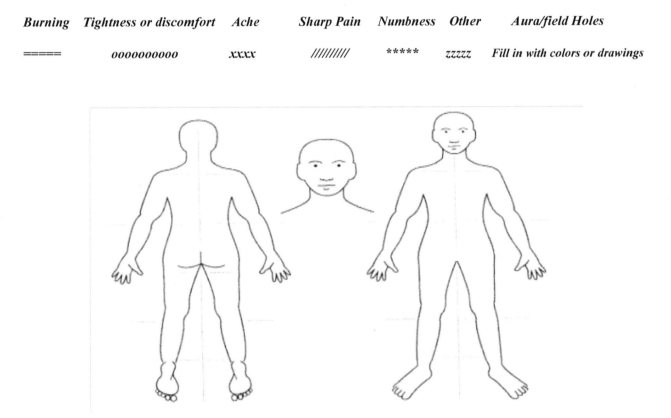

Notes:

Energetic Resonancy & Dousing Form

These forms you can use with your dowsing tool or your body as a dousing rod or energetic resonancy gauge. You can close your eyes or use a soft gaze after doing your body check to get you heart centered and prepared to listen to your body cues for resonancy. This resonancy is what will guide partner energy sessions or self-care sessions. This is the easiest form to use as it is never wrong even if you were way off on what you thought you needed before the session then during the session something else came up, and you got different answers for your after session review

Steps to work with the energetic resonancy and dousing form:

9. Body check

10. Write name & date

11. Choose dowsing or energetic resonancy

12. Picture the person who you are visualizing the dosage for- you or another person

13. Ask their higher source what essence would be best serving to them at this moment?

14. Then run your finger or dousing tool over the CannaEssence & Color Choices form

    a. Mark any that get a yes answers, have a heavy or dragging sensation, holding back from going forward and more. Trust your intuition here and just write down what comes first. You can always do a before and after compare session and see how resonant you were

        i. with your client or self when you are complete

15. Now that you know which essences & colors you need, you will have to figure out the dosing duration in days or months for each essence or color you choose

    a. *To do this, you will need to place your finger on the block you choose & visualize the color or essence and ask your body or the resonancy between you and another's source how long they will need to take this particular essence. Then run your finger over the duration section marking in the essence or color box the duration. Continue to do this for all of your essences or colors*

16. You will follow the above steps for each color and essence with focus on how to best apply the essence or color for your systems or your resonancy partners system

    a. *This is an exercise that can take a bit of practice to feel comfortable doing it as it requires trust in your intuition and the cues that you are getting. These can be extremely subtle, so much so that many folks will dismiss them. That is why the before and after is so cool. As you get to know what's you and what's your resonancy with an essence or color things will become easy and clarified. Just give yourself time, a break and have fun with the exploration!*

CannaEssence^{tm} ENERGETIC RESONANCY & DOUSING FORM

Clients Name:
Practitioner:
Date:

Before or After   session   – circle please

Essences	SB	GC	GG	HB	EB	JB	BB	DP	PK	OG	MK	BJ
Colors	Red	Ora	Yell	Lime	Green	Em	Turq	Blu	Indi	Purp	Vio	Mage
DOSING **Duration**	1	2	3	4	5	6	7	8	9	10	11	12
Days to be used	13	14	15	16	17	18	19	20	21	22	23	24
	25	26	27	28	29	30	31	MORE: 6 weeks 8 weeks 3month				
Frequency *X per day*	1	2	3	4	5	6	7	8	9	10	11	12
Application **Type**	Drops Intern	Auric Infuse	Bath	Lotion cream	Spong FB	Cotton Ball	Lotion	Oil	Aloe Vera	Spray Mist	Compress	Reflex
How to Apply	Full Body	Focus Area	Direct	Pain Zone	Spine	Full Body	Internal Drops					

Chapter 15 Cannabis Energy Medicine Protocols

SELF Heart Chakra Application with the Core 4

Heart Chakra Calibration- Anterior & Posterior (front & back)

1.   Heart space- Anterior (front) - Apply a compress to the front of GREEN to the heart space.

2.   Heart space- Posterior/back apply a compress of VIOLET to the back heart chakra space and along the shoulder blades outlining the "wings" of your light spirit. Apply a compress to the back from T12 through S3, or use the cotton ball method application to the back from T-12 through S3

3.   Side Heart - PURPLE Under armpits and down side of body to floating ribs

4.   Grounded Heart - RED applies to the areas of your genital gender preference

> -Women- RED- Apply directly to the vaginal opening making sure completely to cover the area in a wide circle motions

> -Men-RED- Apply directly to the testicular sac directly in the middle of both your testicles. Or apply to your perineal whichever is calling most to your system

Heart Chakra Transformation Protocol Version #2

The Heart Chakra Transformation is a great protocol to use when you need to balance the front/back & sides of the body with the intention of living from the heart. Use this protocol 1x a week for one month to see transformative effects, therefore raising your PEMS to new heights.

Directions:

1. Perform the body check exercise part 1 & 2

2. Follow the direction for using the application pads. Start first with Green or Abundance.

3. Apply Abundance/Green to the front of the body directly over the heart and the surrounding area. Apply up to the collarbones to the xiphoid process and out to the sides before you get to the underarms. Cover the chest with smooth strokes. Then place used treatment pad on a dish to the side.

4. Empty your treatment cup, by drinking the liquid within

5. Add new warm water to the treatment cup & add 3-6 drops of Purple or Destiny's Calling

6. Apply Destiny's Calling to your underarms to activate and nourish the side heart chakras. Supporting your lion heart. Apply as far down the ribs as feels good to the body

7. Empty your treatment cup, by drinking the liquid within

8. Add new warm water to the treatment cup & add 3-6 drops of Red- Grounding

9. Apply Grounding/red down the spine by using the cotton ball method to apply

    a. Apply red to your root chakra if you did not apply the essence nude

10. Empty your treatment cup, by drinking the liquid within or giving to a plant

    a. Use non-bleached cotton pads to drink without aftertastes

11. Add new warm water to the treatment cup & add 3-6 drops of Violet- Cleansing

12. Apply Cleansing/ violet to the tops of your shoulders

13. Apply Cleansing to the tips of each finger of both hands

14. Go lay down horizontal & warm for at least 45 minutes

15. Perform the body check to see what has shifted

Chapter 16 Energy Center Quiz Answer Key

1:(7pt) Name to the color

                                                        Word Bank

1. Heart   Green

2. 3rd Eye   Indigo   Red

3. Solar plexus   Yellow   Green

4. Root   Red   Indigo

5. Crown   Violet   Violet

6. Sacral   Orange   Yellow

7. Throat   Blue   Orange

                                                       Blue

2:(2 pt) Stability, Grounding, the physical, are traits of

A: Green/ Heart
B: Red/ Root
C: Violet/ Crown
D: None of the above

3:(2pt) What one sub-Chakra did we talk about and the corresponding anatomy

A: Purple / High heart
B: Yellow / Lateral heart
C: Purple / Lateral heart
D: Green / post 3rd Eye

4:(2pt) Spirituality, Wisdom, Understanding Are traits of

A: Violet / crown
B: Green / Heart
C: Red / Root
D None of the above

5:(3pt) List three facts about the heart Chakra

           green   purple   5th chakra

6:(2pt) What two colors support the heart chakra?

A: Violet / Green
B: Green / Purple
C: Purple/Violet
D None of the above

7(2pt) Throat & Crown Chakras are best represented by

A: Truth / Vision
B: Thymus / Thyroid Problems
C: Blue / Violet
D: all of the above

This Page is Intentionally Left Blank

Chapter 17 Cut Me Please – Color Boards

Unlike most books, I want you to cut this book open and utilize the high-quality print resources to get started using Cannabis Energy medicines and VibroChromoTherapy today. Whether or not you own a set of the CannaEssences, you will raise your vibration and self-heal using these wonderful tools of VibroChromoPictoGraphy. Please be mindful of your cutting, so you do not break apart the seam of the book. If you cut along the scissor lines you will have equal sized color boards. I highly suggest you laminate all your color boards to increase their longevity.

LOOK FOR THESE GUIDELINES TO HELP YOU

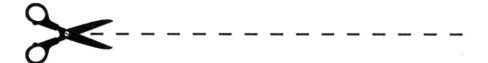

I hope you will enjoy playing with these color boards as much as I do ☺

Cut Outs for VibroChromoTherapy Enhancement Card/Color Boards – Optional

Red

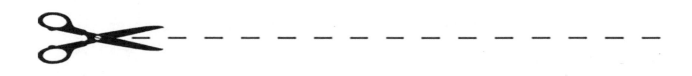

Orange

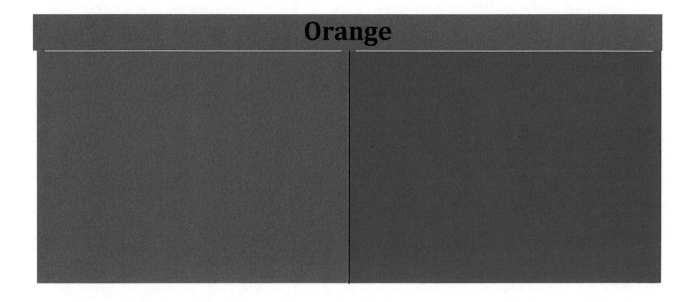

This Page is Intentionally Left Blank

Yellow

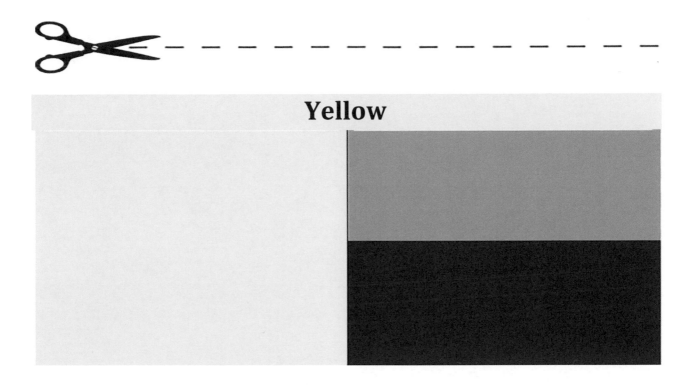

Lime

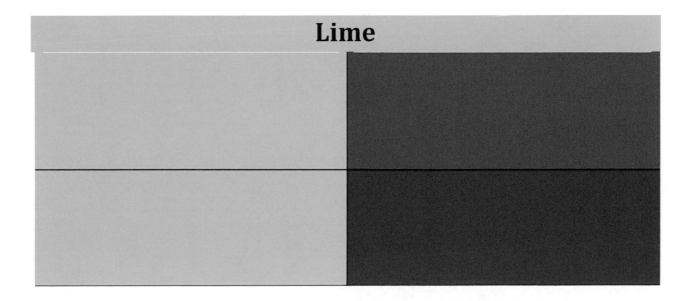

This Page is Intentionally Left Blank

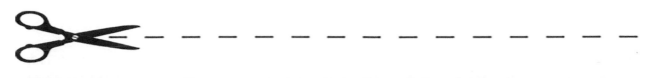

Green

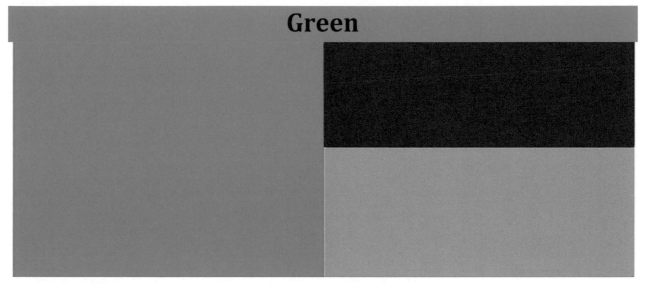

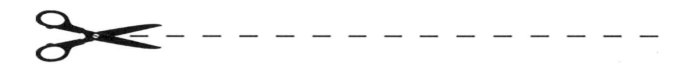

Emerald

This Page is Intentionally Left Blank

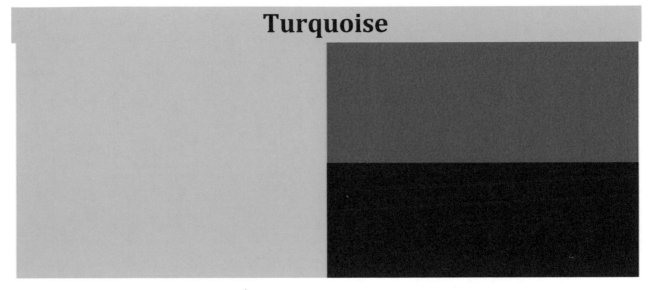

Turquoise

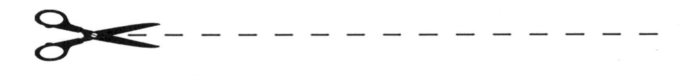

Blue

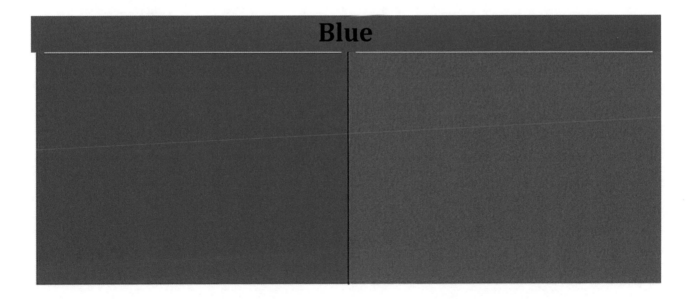

This Page is Intentionally Left Blank

Indigo

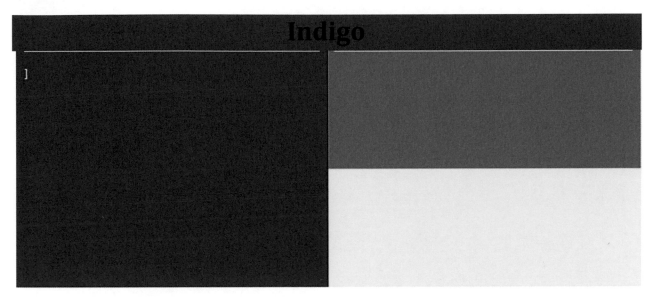

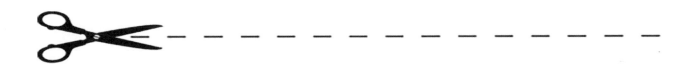

Purple

This Page is Intentionally Left Blank

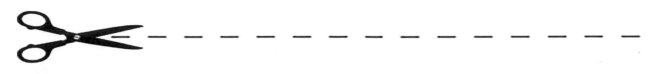

Violet

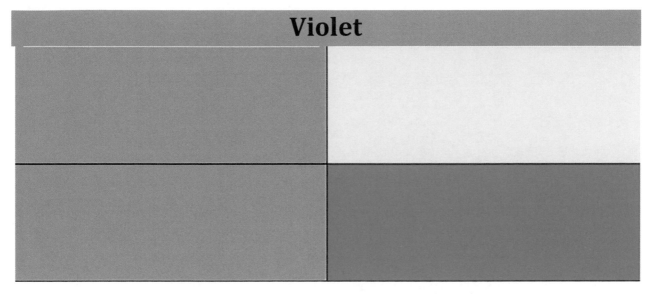

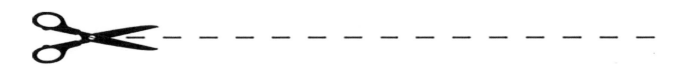

Magenta

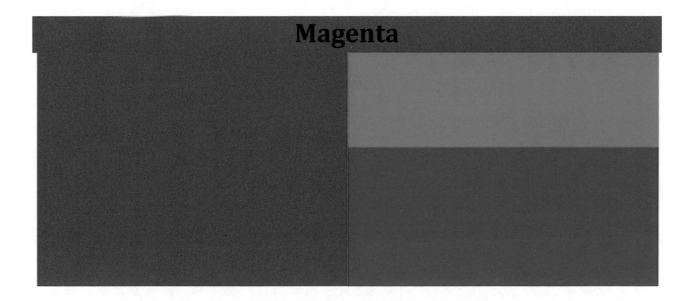

This Page is Intentionally Left Blank

Cut Me First – Cut Outs Master Flower
CannaEssence Color Boards

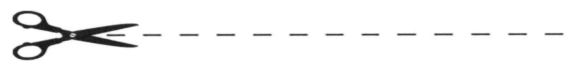

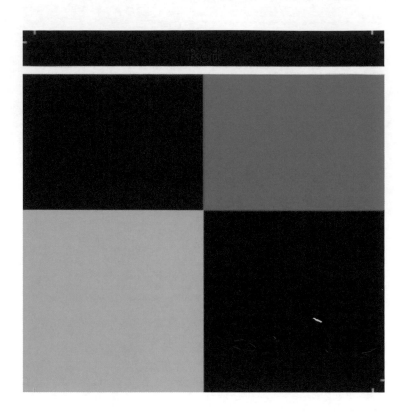

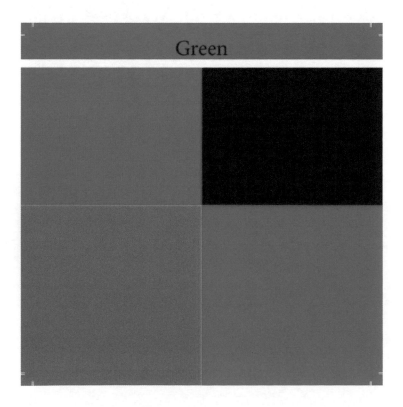

Green

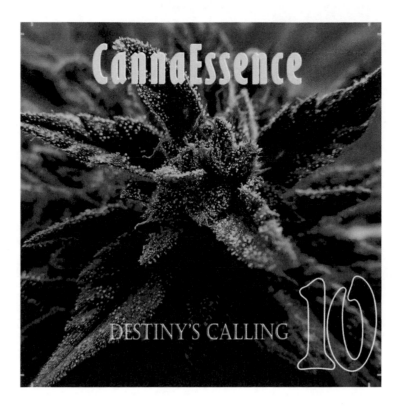

CannaEssence

DESTINY'S CALLING 10

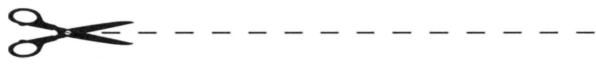

CannaEssence

CLEANSING 11

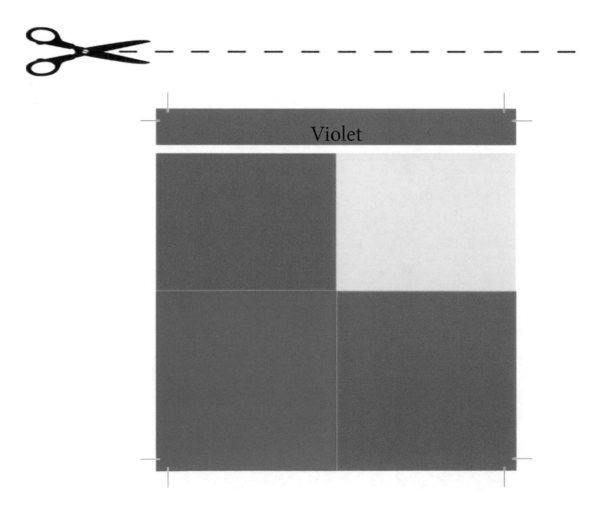

Violet

Coming Soon

Upcoming Books

1. **Cannabis Energy Medicine - Uses and Applications Volume #2**

2. **Cannabis Energy Medicine- Volume #3 – VCT**

3. **Heal Fibromyalgia with Cannabis Energy Medicine Volume #4**

4. **The Science of Cannabis Energy Medicine Volume #5**

5. **Cannabis Massage – The Drug-Free Cannabis Energy Guidebook for Practitioners Volume #6**

6. **Live like a Super Woman – 6 Week Guide to Health & Vitality – Activate Your Superpowers**

7. *Encyclopedia of Quantum Bach Flower Essences - A complete guide to healing your Physical, Emotional, Mental and Spiritual Bodies. A Color and Picture Diagnostic System eBook*

*Note Title may be subject to change. Stay up to date at; www.CannaEssence.org

Distributor Opportunities with CannaEssence

Retail & Practitioner Products

Retail Products to Increase Product Revenue

Spa & Practitioner Display Bottles

1. Grounding - Red

2. Abundance - Green

3. Destiny's Calling- Purple

4. Cleansing - Violet

Spa & Massage Cannabis Energy Medicine

1. Ask your client to choose a picture from the core 4 master flower card.

You will have the master information sheet to tell them why they choose that flower. They will think you are a mind reader, because that is exactly what is going on for them right now.

Pick the Flower You are Most Attracted to

2. Add 6-12 drops to any spa treatment to enhance its effects. Each treatment is custom blended with simplicity.

3. Add 3 drops of flower essence to the tea or water after the session.
Let them know that the flower essences work with acupuncture meridians to help support the PEMS or the Physical, Emotional, Mental & Spiritual wellbeing.

4. Let them know that the flower essence for them can be found in the retail area. If used 2-4 times a day for 7-10 days they will notice a difference in their PEMS. Quicker if they drink enhanced beverages throughout the day and apply the essences to the body 1-5 days. These simple add-ons can increase sales through product revenue. If clients use the essences regularly their PEMS health with increase as well.

About the Author

Jamie Lynn started her journey to vital health through a debilitating chronic illness that resulted in her taking 50 prescribed medications. Jamie was told she would be disabled for life; unable to walk without assistance or live a normal young woman's life without medications and lingering complex problems. After hearing this bleak future, Jamie Lynn was determined to find "another way to heal and become whole." To do so, she went to two full-time schools at the same time to learn as much as she could about human health. She continued to get thirty more degrees, certifications, licenses and diplomas to enlighten her PEMS or Physical, Emotional, Mental, Spiritual bodies. Now 16 medication free years later, Jamie Lynn is an avid mountain climber full of vitality, vision, and vibration.

She uses her experience of hopelessness from diagnoses to help her clients'; specializing in empowering others to heal through PEMS reconnection. Jamie Lynn felt that the balancing of her PEMS is what saved her life and allowed her to regain health; exceeding all the expectations for someone with her conditions. She is a living, breathing miracle.

This passion and understanding are what drove Jamie Lynn to create a product that would support her clients in a powerfully simple way. She wanted to use the most potent tools to create a conscious, sustainable and beautiful product that would serve humanity and the planet alike. Therefore, the CannaEssences were created, then used in the clinical trial and case studies with a focus on chronic conditions like cancer, fibromyalgia, and pain. Jamie Lynn uses the CannaEssences personally in combination with her favorite tools for self-care, cosmetics, and daily maintenance. She blends them into her total health programs to serve her client's vital health.

Jamie Lynn has served as faculty and administration at the North American Institute of Medical Herbalism and the Academy of Natural Therapy. Jamie Lynn has published four books, six magazines and is currently in the process of publishing more books to help people reconnect to their PEMS through the Cannabis and Bach Flower Plant Spirits using vibrational imprints, color therapy, and sacred geometry. She presents workshops in VibroChromoTherapy, VibroChromoPictography, and Cannabis reeducation.

Jamie Lynn graduated from the North American Institute of Medical Herbalism with honors holding Clinical Certifications of Herbalism, Nutrition and Bach Flower Essences. As well as the Metropolitan State College with Two Bachelor certifications: Integrative Therapeutics, Nutrition, and Biology. The Colorado School of Healing Arts with certifications & advanced training in Medical and Oncology Massage Therapy, Neuromuscular & Structural Massage Therapy, Craniosacral and Lymphatic Drainage Therapies, Healing Touch, Trauma Touch Therapy, Polarity. Flora Corona a Certification in Quantum Flower Essences and Color Therapy. Academy of Resonance Therapy with certifications in Quantum Mechanics. As well as completing apprenticeships and mentoring in energetic modalities such as Reiki master, Peruvian & Earth-based medicines. Internships in: Teaching, Pre-Medicine, Gardening, Biofeedback, and Psychiatry.

Contact Information:

Call: 720-316-0196.

Check out my website at www.CannaEssence.org

Email me at Info@CannaEssence.org, Jamie@CannaEssence.org

59965710R00101

Made in the USA
Charleston, SC
16 August 2016